Introduction to Reasoning and Proof

Grades PreK–2

Karren Schultz-Ferrell
Brenda Hammond
Josepha Robles

The Math Process Standards Series
Susan O'Connell, Series Editor

HEINEMANN
Portsmouth, NH

Heinemann
A division of Reed Elsevier Inc.
361 Hanover Street
Portsmouth, NH 03801–3912
www.heinemann.com

Offices and agents throughout the world

The authors and publisher wish to thank those who have generously given permission to reprint borrowed material:

Excerpts from *Principles and Standards for School Mathematics*. Copyright © 2000 by the National Council of Teachers of Mathematics. Reprinted with permission. All rights reserved.

Library of Congress Cataloging-in-Publication Data
Schultz-Ferrell, Karren.
    Introduction to reasoning and proof : grades pre K–2 / Karren Schultz-Ferrell, Brenda Hammond, Josepha Robles.
        p. cm. — (The math process standards series)
    Includes bibliographical references.
    ISBN 978-0-325-01115-8 (alk. paper)
    1. Mathematics—Study and teaching (Preschool)—Standards.
 2. Mathematics—Study and teaching (Preschool)—Activity programs.
 3. Mathematics—Study and teaching (Early childhood)—Standards.
 4. Mathematics—Study and teaching (Early childhood)—Activity programs.
 I. Hammond, Brenda.   II. Robles, Josepha.   III. Title.
    QA135.6.S429 2007
    372.7—dc22   2007016192

Editor: Emily Michie Birch
Production coordinator: Elizabeth Valway
Production service: Matrix Productions, Inc.
Cover design: Night & Day Design
Cover photography: Lauren Robertson
Composition: Publishers' Design and Production Services, Inc.
CD production: Nicole Russell and Marla Berry
Manufacturing: Jamie Carter

Printed in the United States of America on acid-free paper
11   10   09   08   07   ML   1   2   3   4   5

The authors dedicate this work to our families and friends,
whose love sustains us.

To my brother, Fred, and sisters, Nikki and Kriss, with love.
To Carol and Kathy, good friends and teachers.

—KSF

To Al and A.J., and to my brothers, Wendell and Harold, with love.

—BHH

To James and Ariana for their love, patience, and support.

—JR

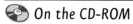 On the CD-ROM

In order to be effective mathematicians, students need to develop understanding of critical math content. They need to understand number and operations, algebra, measurement, geometry, and data analysis and probability. Through continued study of these content domains, students gain a comprehensive understanding of mathematics as a subject with varied and interconnected concepts. As math teachers, we attempt to provide students with exposure to, exploration in, and reflection about the many skills and concepts that make up the study of mathematics.

Even with a deep understanding of math content, however, students may lack important skills that can assist them in their development as effective mathematicians. Along with content knowledge, students need an understanding of the processes used by mathematicians. They must learn to problem solve, communicate their ideas, reason through math situations, prove their conjectures, make connections between and among math concepts, and represent their mathematical thinking. Development of content alone does not provide students with the means to explore, express, or apply that content. As we strive to develop effective mathematicians, we are challenged to develop both students' content understanding and process skills.

The National Council of Teachers of Mathematics (2000) has outlined critical content and process standards in its *Principles and Standards for School Mathematics* document. These standards have become the roadmap for the development of textbooks, curriculum materials, and student assessments. These standards have provided a framework for thinking about what needs to be taught in math classrooms and how various skills and concepts can be blended together to create a seamless math curriculum. The first five standards outline content standards and expectations related to number and operations, algebra, geometry, measurement, and data analysis and probability. The second five standards outline the process goals of problem solving, reasoning and proof, communication, connections, and representations. A strong understanding of these standards empowers teachers to identify and select activities within their curricula to produce powerful learning. The standards provide a vision for what teachers hope their students will achieve.

This book is a part of a vital series designed to assist teachers in understanding the NCTM Process Standards and the ways in which they impact and guide student learning. An additional goal of this series is to provide practical ideas to support teachers as they ensure that the acquisition of process skills has a critical place in their math instruction. Through this series, teachers will gain an understanding of each process standard as well as gather ideas for bringing that standard to life within their math classrooms. It offers practical ideas for lesson development, implementation, and assessment that work with any curriculum. Each book in the series focuses on a critical process skill in a highlighted grade band and all books are designed to encourage reflection about teaching and learning. The series also highlights the interconnected nature of the process and content standards by showing correlations between them and showcasing activities that address multiple standards.

Students who develop an understanding of content skills and cultivate the process skills that allow them to apply that content understanding become effective mathematicians. Our goal as teachers is to support and guide students as they develop both their content knowledge and their process skills, so they are able to continue to expand and refine their understanding of mathematics. This series is a guide for math educators who aspire to teach students more than math content. It is a guide to assist teachers in understanding and teaching the critical processes through which students learn and make sense of mathematics.

Susan O'Connell
Series Editor

ACKNOWLEDGMENTS

This book and the accompanying CD could not have been completed without the encouragement and support of many people. The authors wish to express deep appreciation to all of them.

We extend a special thanks to Sue O'Connell, who saw the vision for this project and initiated our participation, and to Emily Birch, who read and edited this work and advised and encouraged us.

We thank our colleagues, Tanya, Sandy, Lesley, Stacy, Scott, Jackie, Hyon Mi, Deb, Michelle, Liliana, Myrian, Georgiana, and Dorothy who supported this endeavor.

To the students who happily shared their thinking while reasoning about increasingly difficult problems, we extend our most grateful appreciation. This work could not have been completed without their enthusiastic cooperation. We also extend a heartfelt thanks to their parents, who gave us permission to use their pictures and work.

We value the constant support and understanding of friends throughout this undertaking.

To our families, whose love and confidence in us have been a source of strength, we are extremely grateful.

Finally, we wish to applaud our complete confidence in one another. Our ability to approach and complete this project with humor, honesty, and mutual respect saw us through this exciting project and kept our friendship thriving.

NCTM PROCESS STANDARDS
AND EXPECTATIONS *

Problem-Solving Standard

Instructional programs from prekindergarten through grade 12 should enable all students to—

- build new mathematical knowledge through problem solving;

- solve problems that arise in mathematics and in other contexts;

- apply and adapt a variety of appropriate strategies to solve problems;

- monitor and reflect on the process of mathematical problem solving.

Reasoning and Proof Standard

Instructional programs from prekindergarten through grade 12 should enable all students to—

- recognize reasoning and proof as fundamental aspects of mathematics;

- make and investigate mathematical conjectures;

- develop and evaluate mathematical arguments and proofs;

- select and use various types of reasoning and methods of proof.

*Standards are listed with the permission of the National Council of Teachers of Mathematics (NCTM). NCTM does not endorse the content or validity of these alignments.

Communication Standard

Instructional programs from prekindergarten through grade 12 should enable all students to—

- organize and consolidate their mathematical thinking through communication;

- communicate their mathematical thinking coherently and clearly to peers, teachers, and others;

- analyze and evaluate the mathematical thinking and strategies of others;

- use the language of mathematics to express mathematical ideas precisely.

Connections Standard

Instructional programs from prekindergarten through grade 12 should enable all students to—

- recognize and use connections among mathematical ideas;

- understand how mathematical ideas interconnect and build on one another to produce a coherent whole;

- recognize and apply mathematics in contexts outside of mathematics.

Representation Standard

Instructional programs from prekindergarten through grade 12 should enable all students to—

- create and use representations to organize, record, and communicate mathematical ideas;

- select, apply, and translate among mathematical representations to solve problems;

- use representations to model and interpret physical, social, and mathematical phenomena.

NCTM Content Standards and Expectations for Grades PreK–2

NUMBER AND OPERATIONS

	Expectations
Instructional programs from prekindergarten through grade 12 should enable all students to—	**In prekindergarten through 2nd grade all students should—**
Understand numbers, ways of representing numbers, relationships among numbers, and number systems	• count with understanding and recognize "how many" in sets of objects; • use multiple models to develop initial understandings of place value and the base-ten number system; • develop understanding of the relative position and magnitude of whole numbers and of ordinal and cardinal numbers and their connections; • develop a sense of whole numbers and represent and use them in flexible ways, including relating, composing, and decomposing numbers; • connect number words and numerals to the quantities they represent, using various physical models and representations; • understand and represent commonly used fractions, such as 1/4, 1/3, and 1/2.
Understand meanings of operations and how they relate to one another	• understand various meanings of addition and subtraction of whole numbers and the relationship between the two operations; • understand the effects of adding and subtracting whole numbers; • understand situations that entail multiplication and division, such as equal groupings of objects and sharing equally.
Compute fluently and make reasonable estimates	• develop and use strategies for whole-number computations, with a focus on addition and subtraction;

	Expectations
Instructional programs from prekindergarten through grade 12 should enable all students to—	**In prekindergarten through 2nd grade all students should—**
	• develop fluency with basic number combinations for addition and subtraction;
	• use a variety of methods and tools to compute, including objects, mental computation, estimation, paper and pencil, and calculators.

ALGEBRA

	Expectations
Instructional programs from prekindergarten through grade 12 should enable all students to—	**In prekindergarten through 2nd grade all students should—**
Understand patterns, relations, and functions	• sort, classify, and order objects by size, number, and other properties;
	• recognize, describe, and extend patterns such as sequences of sounds and shapes or simple numeric patterns and translate from one representation to another;
	• analyze how both repeating and growing patterns are generated.
Represent and analyze mathematical situations and structures using algebraic symbols	• illustrate general principles and properties of operations, such as commutativity, using specific numbers;
	• use concrete, pictorial, and verbal representations to develop an understanding of invented and conventional symbolic notations.
Use mathematical models to represent and understand quantitative relationships	• model situations that involve the addition and subtraction of whole numbers, using objects, pictures, and symbols.
Analyze change in various contexts	• describe qualitative change, such as a student's growing taller;
	• describe quantitative change, such as a student's growing two inches in one year.

	Expectations
Instructional programs from prekindergarten through grade 12 should enable all students to—	**In prekindergarten through 2nd grade all students should—**
Analyze characteristics and properties of two- and three-dimensional geometric shapes and develop mathematical arguments about geometric relationships	• recognize, name, build, draw, compare, and sort two- and three-dimensional shapes; • describe attributes and parts of two- and three-dimensional shapes; • investigate and predict the results of putting together and taking apart two- and three-dimensional shapes.
Specify locations and describe spatial relationships using coordinate geometry and other representational systems	• describe, name, and interpret relative positions in space and apply ideas about relative position; • describe, name, and interpret direction and distance in navigating space and apply ideas about direction and distance; • find and name locations with simple relationships such as "near to" and in coordinate systems such as maps.
Apply transformations and use symmetry to analyze mathematical situations	• recognize and apply slides, flips, and turns; • recognize and create shapes that have symmetry.
Use visualization, spatial reasoning, and geometric modeling to solve problems	• create mental images of geometric shapes using spatial memory and spatial visualization; • recognize and represent shapes from different perspectives; • relate ideas in geometry to ideas in number and measurement; • recognize geometric shapes and structures in the environment and specify their location.

MEASUREMENT

	Expectations
Instructional programs from prekindergarten through grade 12 should enable all students to—	**In prekindergarten through 2nd grade all students should—**
Understand measurable attributes of objects and the units, systems, and processes of measurement	• recognize the attributes of length, volume, weight, area, and time; • compare and order objects according to these attributes; • understand how to measure using nonstandard and standard units; • select an appropriate unit and tool for the attribute being measured.
Apply appropriate techniques, tools, and formulas to determine measurements	• measure with multiple copies of units of the same size, such as paper clips laid end to end; • use repetition of a single unit to measure something larger than the unit, for instance, measuring the length of a room with a single meterstick; • use tools to measure; • develop common referents for measures to make comparisons and estimates.

DATA ANALYSIS AND PROBABILITY

	Expectations
Instructional programs from prekindergarten through grade 12 should enable all students to—	**In prekindergarten through 2nd grade all students should—**
Formulate questions that can be addressed with data and collect, organize, and display relevant data to answer them	• pose questions and gather data about themselves and their surroundings; • sort and classify objects according to their attributes and organize data about the objects; • represent data using concrete objects, pictures, and graphs.
Select and use appropriate statistical methods to analyze data	• describe parts of the data and the set of data as a whole to determine what the data show.
Develop and evaluate inferences and predictions that are based on data	• discuss events related to students' experiences as likely or unlikely.
Understand and apply basic concepts of probability	

The Reasoning and Proof Standard

The ability to reason systematically and carefully develops when students are encouraged to make conjectures, are given time to search for evidence to prove or disprove them, and are expected to explain and justify their ideas.

—National Council of Teachers of Mathematics,
Principles and Standards for School Mathematics

Why Focus on Reasoning and Proof?

The mathematics classroom of the past might have been one of the quietest places in the school. Opportunities for students to explain thinking and reasoning were rarely offered. In today's classrooms, however, reasoning is viewed as a necessary process for ensuring that students understand mathematics concepts and skills. "Many mathematicians consider the NCTM standard concerning reasoning and proof to be its most important" (Chapin, O'Connor, and Canavan Anderson 2003, 78). Students benefit when we provide them with opportunities to explain thinking and reasoning not only through discourse but also through the recording of representations (e.g., charts, graphs, drawings, diagrams, etc.) of mathematical thinking. Students should also be given opportunities to reflect on their thinking and reasoning through writing. All of these experiences help students extend their thinking, solidify understandings about concepts and skills, and learn the different ways their classmates think about, reason with, and solve mathematics problems and situations.

Although we realize the importance of questioning our students about their thinking when problem-solving errors are evident, many of us do not realize how critical it is to question students about their mathematical thinking and to discuss their reasoning with them at all times. Listening to students as they explain their reasoning in thinking about a mathematical idea gives us valuable information about what they know and are able to do. Students' strengths and misconceptions are revealed, which provides us with information that will help us plan instruction to meet the needs of all of our students. In addition to helping us gain information about students, our questioning delivers important messages to students: their ideas are valued and important; mathematics is less about memorization and more about reasoning; and what they are learning should make sense (Burns 1997).

As previously noted, reasoning can be expressed through representations as well. We must encourage young children to record how they are thinking about the math they are learning by drawing representations of these ideas. These representations become evidence of learning that can be shared later with families. When students become confident in explaining and representing thinking and reasoning, then they are more able to write about their reasoning. When we emphasize reasoning in our classrooms, then our students will become engaged in different types of reasoning, and they will begin to understand how to express acceptable mathematical explanations.

What Is the Reasoning and Proof Standard?

The National Council of Teachers of Mathematics (NCTM) has recommended standards that can be used as a resource and a guide for teachers as we plan and create instructional lessons and activities to develop our students' understandings about mathematics. The first five standards are the mathematical content goals: number and operations, algebra, geometry, measurement, and data analysis and probability. The next five standards address the processes by which students explore and use mathematics as well as develop understandings about mathematics concepts and skills. The process standards should be embedded throughout our instructional program.

> Instructional programs from prekindergarten through grade 12 should enable all students to—
>
> ▪ recognize reasoning and proof as fundamental aspects of mathematics;
>
> ▪ make and investigate mathematical conjectures;
>
> ▪ develop and evaluate mathematical arguments and proof; and
>
> ▪ select and use various types of reasoning and methods of proof. (NCTM 2000, 56)

This book explores ways to assist young learners in extending their thinking, deepening understandings, and making sense of mathematics through the process standard of reasoning and proof.

Developing Skills and Attitudes

"Reasoning mathematically is a habit of mind, and like all habits, it must be developed through consistent use in many contexts" (NCTM 2000, 56). The ability to reason develops over time with multiple experiences. We must provide our students with daily opportunities to reason about the mathematics they are learning. It must become a part of the way we teach in order for our students to become proficient in their ability to reason.

Establishing a classroom environment that is both respectful and supportive is the first step in helping our students become comfortable enough to offer explanations of mathematical thinking and reasoning with confidence. Ground rules are needed to create a classroom climate in which students listen respectfully to one another during mathematics discussions. Students must feel safe when expressing their thinking and sharing their own ideas for examination. They will not contribute to a discussion if they feel their ideas will be made fun of or dismissed quickly. We must be consistent with our expectations of behaviors during these discussions.

This also involves the expectation that all students will listen to what others say, which allows them to participate more actively in an ongoing discussion. Students need our support in order to develop the skills necessary to participate in teacher-to-student, student-to-student, and student-to-teacher discourse. They must have daily opportunities to talk and reason about mathematics if we want them to be able to then represent and write about mathematical reasoning.

Presenting tasks to students that are open-ended and rich in context provides students with opportunities to develop reasoning skills. When we present problems to our students that can be solved in more than one way, or that have more than one correct answer, it promotes talk about thinking and reasoning. Problems that cause students to stretch their thinking are a must. This book addresses all the considerations introduced in this section, as well as others, to help you begin to implement the reasoning and proof standard into your daily instruction.

How This Book Will Help You

This book is designed to help you better understand the NCTM Process Standard of reasoning and proof for students in prekindergarten through grade 2. It explains how these students' early reasoning abilities prepare them for more complex reasoning in the intermediate grades and beyond. Specific types of reasoning are described, and student dialogues are provided throughout the book to model how primary students use these different ways to reason. The teachers facilitating these student dialogues model critical questioning that promotes rich discussions in which students are reasoning about the mathematics they are learning.

We share tools and strategies that will help your students think deductively and inductively in an organized manner. These tools and strategies will support students in solving complicated problems and are included for you on the CD. We discuss how you can provide reasoning experiences for your students in which they will begin to make conjectures about important mathematical ideas and relationships. Primary students should be encouraged to support their conjectures by providing explanations and justifications. Student dialogues are provided to demonstrate how children begin to formulate conjectures and then explain their reasoning with informal mathematical arguments.

We note several strategies that teachers can use to support students in developing reasoning skills, and activities that promote reasoning are included on the CD. The activities provided on the CD do not list specific grade levels because the activities have been formatted so that you can modify them to meet the needs, interests, and skills levels of all your students. We describe how to do this in the "About the CD-ROM" section near the end of this book. We encourage you to choose activities that fit your content and instructional goals. Many of the problems and activities demonstrated for you in the student dialogues throughout the book are on the CD. You will find these activities to be both engaging and challenging for your students, and facilitating discussions with your students about the problem solving within the activities will support their reasoning skills. These discussions can occur either while your students are solving the tasks as a whole group or by discussing students' problem solving and reasoning after they have completed an activity. In addition to the CD activities, you will find a listing of resources that will help your students make sense of mathematics, promote reasoning, and strengthen their mathematics concepts and skills. Also included on the CD are several rubrics that will be helpful in assessing your students' development of reasoning skills: a rubric you can use to monitor your students' development of reasoning skills and a rubric students can use to monitor their reasoning progress.

As mentioned earlier, examples of student discourse demonstrate how young students reason about important mathematical ideas and relationships and serve as a model for how to facilitate discussions that promote reasoning in your own classroom. These examples demonstrate how students are reasoning about a variety of mathematics concepts and skills. In addition, examples of student work are presented that provide another glimpse into students' thinking as their reasoning and proof skills develop. Practical tips and ideas are shared in the "Classroom-Tested Tip" boxes to help you implement the ideas explored in the chapters. Following each chapter, you will find several discussion questions included for you to reflect on the content of the chapter, either alone or with a group of your colleagues.

Chapter 5 discusses how the process standard of reasoning and proof is supported by the remaining process standards: problem solving, communication, representation, and connections. We discuss how students' reasoning helps them make vital connections to their everyday lives, other concepts in math, as well as other discipline areas such as reading, science, and social studies. We share ideas for how to provide students with meaningful tasks that connect reasoning to all the process standards. In Chapter 6, a variety of ways to assess students' reasoning skills are examined. After we have explored the reasoning and proof standard in depth, you will see how it relates to the different content areas in mathematics in Chapter 7, "Reasoning and Proof Across the Content Standards."

The role of communication in supporting students' reasoning has been stressed several times in this chapter, especially communicating reasoning through discourse. It is important to remember that we cannot expect our students to write about mathematical reasoning if they have not talked about it first. Students' ability to communicate their thinking and reasoning through writing as well as through pictorial and symbolic representations is examined in various chapters, and examples of student work have been included throughout the book.

We hope this book will enhance your understanding of the reasoning and proof standard and provide you with practical ideas and strategies that will help develop your students' reasoning and proof skills. When we grow in our understandings about reasoning and proof, so will our students.

Students who leave the elementary grades with a mathematics education that has focused on mathematical reasoning are students who can count on their own thinking and are willing and able to investigate new problem situations for themselves. (Stiff 1999, 12)

Questions for Discussion

1. Did mathematics make sense to you when you were in school? Were you ever asked to explain how you solved a problem? How could your past experiences and attitudes about reasoning affect how you think young students are able to reason?

2. If students state the correct answer but cannot explain why the answer makes sense mathematically, what questions might you have about your students' understanding? How might this inability to explain and reason about mathematics present difficulties later in school?

3. What attitudes or dispositions are crucial for explaining one's thinking and reasoning? How does the atmosphere in the classroom affect students' abilities to develop reasoning?

4. Reflect on the quote included at the end of this chapter by yourself or with colleagues. Compare students who learn mathematics through the process of reasoning to students who learn mathematics through only procedures. How are the two types of learning different? How might students' understanding of mathematics be affected if they only learn procedurally?

1

Creating a Learning Environment That Promotes Reasoning and Proof

Mathematical reasoning develops in classrooms where students are encouraged to put forth their own ideas for examination.

—National Council of Teachers of Mathematics,
Principles and Standards for School Mathematics

Our Attitude Toward Mathematics

Perhaps the most important factor in creating a classroom atmosphere that encourages thinking and reasoning is our attitude toward mathematics. "How a teacher views mathematics and its learning affects that teacher's teaching practice, which ultimately affects not only what the students learn but how they view themselves as mathematics learners" (National Research Council 2001, 132). Teachers who enjoy mathematics tend to have students who also like mathematics.

As your students begin to share how they are thinking and reasoning, you will discover that there is a diverse range of reasoning among them. Students often resort to other means of reasoning about a problem in order to solve it when they do not understand how to complete an algorithm. This is a student's attempt at making sense of mathematics in a way that is not traditionally taught, and this type of reasoning should be respected. When we honor each student's unique approach to reasoning about mathematics, then our students know their creative and critical thinking is important and valued. We must instill confidence in students so that they are ready for the challenges we offer them—challenges that will develop and strengthen their reasoning abilities. In creating a classroom that is a mathematics community, we must show our students that we value mathematics, that we want it to make sense to them, and that reasoning is central to everything we do.

A Safe, Supportive, and Respectful Classroom

In order for students to be comfortable in communicating their mathematical thinking and reasoning, a learning environment must be in place that supports this openness. A student's classroom can be described as a home away from home, so it is natural that we would want to create a classroom atmosphere that provides support and allows our students to feel comfortable. If students feel their ideas will be criticized or made fun of, they will not be willing to share how they are thinking and reasoning about mathematics. To create a classroom environment that promotes reasoning, we must first establish expectations that ensure a supportive environment where students can talk confidently about their thinking and reasoning. These expectations must be clearly understood by all students and consistently reinforced throughout the school year.

It is equally important that we establish a respectful classroom environment. We want our students to know that everyone in the classroom has a right to be heard and that everyone's thinking and reasoning will be considered in a respectful manner. Along with this right for ideas to be heard and considered, we want our students to know there is an expectation that everyone will listen to others' thinking and reasoning. Listening to their classmates carefully will begin to assist students in understanding one another's reasoning and ideas. When students are actively engaged in listening, it enables them to more fully participate in ongoing discussions. As your students begin to share their reasoning, expect that there will be students who disagree with others' thinking. When disagreements occur, the challenge must be accompanied by an explanation that is offered respectfully. The establishment of a safe, supportive, and respectful classroom environment is the first step in setting the stage for reasoning and proof.

CLASSROOM-TESTED TIP

The following suggestions will help you support your students in developing their listening skills:

- Establish a routine that prompts students to get into an effective listening position. Many teachers implement rhymes, chants, songs, or a signal to do this.

- Remind students to wait until the student who is speaking has finished before they begin to talk.

- Present opportunities for students to ask questions after a student has finished speaking. This allows students to clarify anything the speaker has said.

- Expect students to repeat another student's reasoning in their own words to help them better understand what the speaker has shared. For example, "Morgan, please explain what Nick just said."

- Model good listening skills as you listen to your students. When children feel their ideas are being listened to, they will be more likely to listen to you and other classmates.

Engaging and Challenging Mathematics

What else can we do to support our students as they develop reasoning skills? We must choose appropriate tasks that are both engaging and thought provoking for our students—problems that are rich in context, meaningful and relevant to young students' everyday lives, and provide challenging experiences. Consider the following problem, for example:

> My brother's birthday is soon.
> I am sending cupcakes and brownies.
> I can only send a total of ten in the box.
> How many cupcakes and how many brownies could I send?

Not only will this problem elicit multiple solutions from students, it will also require students to think logically about the mathematics involved to determine the possible combinations of cupcakes and brownies. Rich, or non-routine, problems such as this one encourage students to apply a variety of strategies such as making an organized list, completing a chart, or using representations to arrive at a solution.

Students in a first-grade classroom grappled with this problem. The teacher had written the problem on chart paper and posted it on the blackboard. After introducing the problem to her students, she asked them to think about how many cupcakes and brownies could be sent. She then gave them time to talk to a nearby student about what they were thinking. As students were sharing their ideas with one another, the teacher listened to various students as they discussed possible solutions with their partner. Then she facilitated a student discussion. Please note that in the following dialogue, different students responded throughout the discussion although student names are not indicated. This is the organization used in all of the student dialogues in this book.

TEACHER: What do you think? I can only send a total of ten cupcakes and brownies in the box. What can I send?
STUDENT: You can send five cupcakes and five brownies.
TEACHER: Tell us how you figured that out.
STUDENT: Well, I know that 5 and 5 is 10. Five fingers on each of my hands equal ten fingers!

Before asking students to share additional ideas, the teacher introduced a chart as a strategy to help students organize their thinking by recording the combinations of cupcakes and brownies suggested by students. The chart had two columns: one column for recording cupcakes and the other for brownies. Figure 1–1 shows this chart along with students' recorded combinations. A student recorded the possible combinations as the discussion continued.

TEACHER: Does anyone have a different idea? Remember I can only send ten.
STUDENT: I think eight cupcakes and two brownies.
TEACHER: Why do you think that is a way I could send them?

Figure 1–1 *Students record the different combinations for 10 cupcakes and brownies.*

STUDENT: When I put all my fingers down to make eight, there's two leftovers, and when I put the two fingers with the other eight it makes ten in all.

TEACHER: Thank you. We'll add that to our chart. Now we have two ways.

STUDENT: You could do seven brownies and three cupcakes.

TEACHER: Explain how you know that makes ten.

STUDENT: I heard *(student)* say eight and two were ten. So I thought I could use seven and three instead. They're close to eight and two, and they work!

TEACHER: Do you know that for sure?

STUDENT: I knew you'd ask me that so I checked! I said seven and *(student then puts up three fingers one at a time)* eight, nine, ten!

STUDENT: I think you should send nine cupcakes and one brownie. I know it's right because my brother is nine and when I count on from nine one time, it's ten.

STUDENT: I think your brother wants seven cupcakes and three brownies.

TEACHER: Wait, I see we have seven and three on our chart already. What do you all think?

STUDENT: They're different. Cupcakes are better than brownies. I'd want more cupcakes.

TEACHER: So seven cupcakes and three brownies is a different way to fill my box from seven brownies and three cupcakes? *(All students agree.)*

TEACHER: Who else has an idea?

STUDENT: Two cupcakes and eight brownies.

TEACHER: *(Student records 2 and 8 on the chart.)* I see on our chart we now have eight and two; two and eight. Are these different if we don't think about the cupcakes and brownies?

STUDENT: They both equal ten, but the numbers are in different places. They traded places!

TEACHER: Oh, so we can turn the numbers around and still have ten? *(Students agree.)* Does this always work?

STUDENT: We did it on three and seven and seven and three!

STUDENT: We can have one and nine and nine and one then! You just switch the sides like *(student)* said.

TEACHER: So you're saying when you switch the numbers around, you still get the same answer. How cool! Switching the numbers around is like turning them around.

STUDENT: Do we have all the ways?

TEACHER: Hmmmm, I'd like you to work with a partner to see if we have all the ways. You may use the connecting cubes to help you do this.

Because six and four and four and six were not named as combinations for ten cupcakes and brownies, the teacher decided it would be beneficial for students to work in pairs to continue working on this problem. She did not tell her students that more combinations were possible. Doing so would have deprived them of the opportunity to think more deeply about the problem. In a traditional classroom, students often focus on the teacher's facial expressions or *yes* or *no* responses too much, which inhibits them from thinking and reasoning. This teacher was wisely allowing her students' thinking to continue.

To facilitate further exploration of the problem, students were given two colors of connecting cubes and asked to make all the combinations for ten. This would allow them to concretely represent the combinations listed on the chart as well as find more combinations. Students used brown cubes to represent brownies and white cubes to represent cupcakes. They made "sticks" out of the cubes by connecting them together, which represented the different combinations of cupcakes and brownies (e.g., a connected stick of two white cubes and eight brown cubes). After students had sufficient time to further investigate the problem, the teacher asked them to return to the front of the room.

TEACHER: What did you find out? Did we think of all the ways to send cupcakes and brownies?

STUDENT: We made the ways on the chart. That helped us.

STUDENT: We did, too. We thought we told them all. Then we thought maybe six works. So we made six and then counted up to ten. We counted up four times. So six and four make ten.

STUDENT: We got six and four and then switched them. We like turning the numbers around.

TEACHER: What do you think now? Do we have all the combinations for cupcakes and brownies? *(Students nod or say yes.)*

TEACHER: How can we be certain all the combinations have been found?

STUDENT: We lined our cubes up to check. They look like stairs now. That's why we tried four and six. *(See Figure 1–2.)*

Figure 1–2 *A student's representation of "stairs" that helped him verify he had found all the possible combinations for ten.*

TEACHER: Tell us more about what you did. Why do you think arranging the cubes so they look like stairs helps you know you have all the combinations?

STUDENT: The steps go all the way up to ten! We started with one white cube *(and nine brown cubes)*. Next we put two white and eight brown. The cupcakes' part of the cubes *(the white cubes)* keeps getting bigger all the way up.

STUDENT: Yeah, when we did that we saw that part of the stairs were missing! That's when we tried six white and four brown.

TEACHER: What does everyone else think?

The discussion continued as students explained how they knew all the combinations had been found. The connecting cube sticks were a concrete representation of students' thinking and reasoning about this problem. Students were reasoning about the relationship of part-part-whole, a critical concept about number, when they explained and justified how they knew they had all of the possible combinations for ten. This simple problem was challenging and generated a rich discussion that helped develop students' reasoning skills and understanding of the mathematics in the task. It is also a problem that can be easily differentiated based on your students' abilities. For example, a kindergarten teacher used the same problem but adjusted the total amount of cupcakes and brownies. In Figure 1–3, a kindergarten student represents two different combinations for five cupcakes and brownies.

Figure 1–3 *A kindergarten student's representation of two different combinations for five cupcakes and brownies.*

The teacher of this first-grade class supported her students' developing reasoning abilities as she guided them through the problem-solving process and in her facilitation of the student discussion in these ways:

- She posted the problem on the board so that students could revisit it throughout the problem-solving process.

- She used a problem students could solve using different strategies. This problem also generated multiple answers. A problem of this type helps build students' number sense.

- She expected students to explain how they got their answer. Talking about strategies helps students strengthen their reasoning abilities.

- She gave students wait time during the student discussion. This time allowed students to think about the question being asked and to formulate their response.

- She asked probing questions to help students clarify their thinking and reasoning.

- She helped students make connections to similar ideas and informally discover generalizations (e.g., the turn-around facts).

Choosing tasks that engage students in reasoning may at first be challenging. Consider the following when planning your instructional lessons:

- Choose tasks that are interesting for your students to think about, those that come from their everyday lives. Students' natural curiosity about the world can easily be the driving force in a mathematics task or investigation that is embedded with reasoning opportunities. Consider tasks that are directly related to your students' interests such as animals, nature, games, distribution of materials in preparation of a lesson or snack, exploring a problem that arises from the reading of a story, and important events such as birthdays, field trips, assemblies, or class parties.

- Choose tasks that encourage multiple perspectives and representations. This helps students to reason about mathematical ideas and relationships in different ways and allows them to consider others' views. The cupcake and brownie task is an example of this.

- Present tasks that are not easily solved but within your students' abilities. This promotes students' persistence in problem solving. Provide directions for a problem-solving activity. However, do not model any methods for solving the problem. Allow students to work through the problem in their own way. Young students have not been exposed to traditional algorithms and therefore will solve problems using self-generated strategies that make sense to them.

- Introduce tools and/or strategies throughout the year that will help support your students in organizing their thinking about a problem, such as recording on a chart, making a table or a list, finding a pattern, drawing a picture or diagram, or a guess and check method.

- She introduced a chart as a way for students to organize their thinking in order to solve the problem.

The accompanying CD provides activities and tasks such as the cupcake and brownie problem that will actively engage your students in meaningful and challenging mathematics. These activities support students' ability to think more deeply about a variety of mathematics concepts and skills as well as develop their reasoning skills. They are extremely beneficial in motivating students to talk meaningfully about the math they are learning. Your facilitation of these discussions is critical for increasing students' understanding of mathematics and developing their reasoning abilities.

Here are several ways to actively engage students in a discussion:

- Think–pair–share is a strategy that is effective in promoting student talk. It was first developed by Professor Frank Lyman at the University of Maryland in 1981. Students are given about thirty seconds to think quietly about a question that has been asked. This time for students to silently think in order to develop and organize their ideas is an important component of the strategy because it enhances student responses to questions. Each student then pairs with another student to talk about what she was thinking regarding the question (about thirty to sixty seconds). This brief discussion between partners gives students an opportunity to share ideas, clarify each other's thinking, and even challenge and ask questions of one another. Students will be more willing to take risks and share mathematical thinking and reasoning with the class after they have already discussed their ideas with a partner. Students then share ideas with the whole group for about two to three minutes. They either share what they were thinking or something they discussed with their partner. It is important that they be able to share their partner's thinking and reasoning as well as their own. Think-pair-share is also useful when few students are participating in the discussion. We can ask the question again for students to discuss with a partner, and then come back together to continue the discussion. Students often feel more comfortable talking in a whole group after they have processed a question in this manner.

- Reflect back something you observed as students were working. For example, "When you worked on your problem, I noticed that you made two towers of cubes. How did that help you solve the problem?" By reflecting students' actions, we have provided them with a concrete example they can use as they explain their thinking.

- Ask students to describe work that is represented in a drawing.

- Designate a "mathematician's chair" for your students to sit in as they share their thinking and reasoning.

Questioning

Another consideration to think about when supporting students as they develop reasoning skills is the types of questions we ask. Students will be denied the opportunity to reason if the only questions we ask are those that merely require one-word answers. However, questions that require students to ponder about mathematical ideas encourage reasoning, and asking good questions also facilitates productive learning. Here are examples of questions that encourage students to think and reason:

- How do you know? (Ask this question even when students give a correct answer.)

- Is there a different way to solve this problem?

- How can you be sure?

- Why do you think this is the answer?

- What strategy helped you in playing the game? How did this strategy help you? (For kindergarten students ask, "Did you have a plan for playing the game? How did it help you?)

- How are _____ and _____ alike? How are they different?

Although questions that elicit one-word answers are appropriate at times, questions that require students to think and reason about mathematics should be the focus in every lesson. Ask questions that allow students to reflect about the mathematics they are learning. These daily experiences support students as they begin to develop their ability to make conjectures or justify their reasoning. Asking effective questions promotes students' use of critical thinking while helping them learn to establish relationships and make meaningful connections. The following questions also help students see that explanations can be supported or refuted by evidence:

- Why is this right? Will it work every time?

- If we try this with more problems, will it still work?

- Why does (student's) explanation make sense to you?

- What would happen if you . . . ?

- How will you convince us this is true?

Explain to students the changes that will be occurring during your mathematics discussions. Young children need to know that you will be asking questions to find out how they are thinking about the mathematics they are learning. This helps them to understand your expectations and to realize that talking about their thinking and reasoning will improve their understanding of the mathematics being taught. It is important to keep in mind that sharing thinking and ideas in mathematics may be uncomfortable at first for many students. Some students may take longer to feel confident enough to do this. It is a gradual process.

Choose one or two questions to focus on in the beginning, and then as you and your students become comfortable with those questions, expand on the types of questions you ask. When you model good questioning and demonstrate how you want your students to participate in discussions, they will begin to ask the same questions of their classmates and become more comfortable contributing to class discussions. Eventually you want your students to be comfortable asking questions of you and of each other.

CLASSROOM-TESTED TIP

Keep the following considerations in mind when choosing questions to ask students:

■ Choose questions that require students to do more than recite a fact from memory or say yes or no. Questions that cause students to question their own thinking will demand more from them cognitively and will develop stronger mathematical understanding. Asking, "How can we find the total of eight and five in two different ways?" requires students to think more deeply than they would if they were simply asked, "What is eight plus five?" which generates only a one-word answer.

■ Ask probing questions after students have answered the initial question. These questions stimulate students' thinking and present you with more information about how they are thinking. Probing encourages students to think about their thinking and provides an opportunity for them to uncover any errors in their original reasoning, which will help them further clarify their thinking. Even if a response is correct, a probing question might uncover a misconception a student has about the mathematics involved. Examples of probing questions include "What did you find out when you subtracted?" "Do you think it works every time?" and "Would that work with this problem?"

■ Choose questions that elicit two or more acceptable answers, or those that encourage students to use a variety of strategies in problem solving. The cupcake and brownie task in this chapter demonstrates this type of questioning.

■ Choose questions that help students make connections in mathematics, such as "How does addition relate to subtraction?" and "How would understanding addition help us to subtract?"

■ Model questions that strengthen students' self-monitoring skills. It is important that students know when their answers are correct. Questions such as "How did you know you were right?" and "Why does that answer make sense to you?" model the self-monitoring process for students.

Additional Factors That Promote Reasoning

Other considerations can help create a classroom environment that promotes thinking and reasoning. Each of the following ideas will be discussed in more detail in a later chapter.

Discourse

Make it a priority for your students to talk daily with you and their classmates about the mathematics concepts and skills they are learning, which helps them not only to internalize the mathematics they are learning but also to obtain a deeper understanding of it. A language approach to mathematics not only empowers students; it also supports their involvement and encourages them to take risks. Use words and phrases such as *not, if . . . then, because, some, all, or, never*, and *probably* when appropriate in your discussions with students or during daily routines. For example, when students line up to go to lunch, ask students who are *not* wearing blue to line up first. This approach allows students to become familiar with the language of logic and reasoning.

To generate productive discussions, ask questions that cause students to think about the mathematics at hand. Your role is to guide these discussions. An important benefit of discourse is that in order for students to express their thinking in words, they must first reflect on and then clarify their thinking. And when students listen to their classmates' thinking and reasoning, it enhances their own learning. An added benefit of student discussions is the multiple opportunities we are presented to informally gather information about what our students know and are able to do. These daily discussions with our students about their thinking and reasoning are ongoing informal assessments that become an integral part of our classroom instruction.

CLASSROOM-TESTED TIP

Incorrect or Flawed Reasoning

Incorrect or flawed reasoning will occur when your students begin to contribute more of their thinking in daily discussions. We cannot expect that primary students' reasoning will be flawless or completely developed. As students begin to reason about the mathematics they are learning, they must understand that it is acceptable to reflect on, analyze, and rethink others' reasoning, especially reasoning that is flawed. All students should know what it is like to think through reasoning that does not work or make sense.

Treat these moments as learning opportunities for both you and your students. The flaws in a student's reasoning often reveal misconceptions he has as well as those of other students in the group. It is extremely beneficial to allow students time to think through flawed reasoning. Convey to students that making errors because of misunderstandings is part of the reasoning process and that these misconceptions will be examined with the intent of learning from them.

Ask additional questions to probe for clarification, which helps students examine their thinking more closely and gives other students the opportunity to analyze the flaws in their classmates' reasoning. Students should be encouraged to revise any flawed reasoning about problem solving, to make new conjectures, and to explain justifications.

Recording Sheets

Encourage young students to draw pictures to explain their thinking and justify their solutions. A recording sheet allows students to reflect on the mathematics completed, and it provides them with the evidence that is needed to formulate a conjecture and/or develop and justify mathematical arguments. Many of the activities contained on the CD encourage students to record representations of their work as they solve the tasks. These activities also ask students to record their thinking and reasoning about the mathematics in the task.

Writing

When students write about mathematics, it helps them to make sense of what they are learning. They must organize their thinking in order to record these understandings and reflections. Students' written responses also provide information we can use to assess their understanding. The types of writing products vary; the most popular are journals or logs. Writing is an excellent tool for students in grades 1 and 2 to utilize in order to explain their thinking and reasoning, and it can be used for different purposes and formats. Younger students can participate as a group to dictate to you their understanding of the day's mathematics problem-solving activity.

The feedback we provide to students about their writing products is important. Providing informational feedback that is specific, supportive, and honest is critical if we want students to develop clear mathematics understanding. This feedback is especially important when students' reasoning does not make sense or is flawed. Feedback that enables a student to further reflect on his thinking is far more beneficial than a message that simply states, "Almost there!"

CLASSROOM-TESTED TIP

Here are several ways to incorporate reasoning in students' writing activities:

- After completing a problem, students write to explain why the answer makes sense.

- At the conclusion of a mathematics lesson, students write a letter to an absent student to explain the reasoning and problem solving used in the day's mathematics task. Younger students could collectively write a letter with the teacher.

- Students write to explain reasoning in describing a mathematical relationship such as the result of adding two odd numbers.

- Students write to explain their understanding of a counting strategy used in solving a problem such as counting on or counting back.

Wait Time

Students need time to organize their thinking and to formulate an explanation of their solution before answering a question. Before beginning to use wait time with your students, explain that you will be waiting before expecting them to respond to any question you ask. You want them to know that this will help them think about the question asked. It is essential that all students have the same amount of wait time. Wait about ten seconds after asking the whole class a question. When you call on a specific student, provide that student with additional time to organize her thinking before expecting her to provide a response. This gives a student time to think through a question and time to express her thinking and reasoning in words.

Wait time is a beneficial expectation for us as well! After a student has responded to a question, give yourself five to ten seconds to think about the student's answer and how you will respond to it. This time allows you to think about any follow-up or probing questions that will continue to guide a productive discussion. Wait time allows young students to realize that thoughtful explanations are valued more than quick responses.

Probing Questions

Ask questions that encourage students to add more detail to explanations, thus revealing more of what they understand about the mathematics they are learning. This is an important benefit for other students as well. Once students have observed you modeling probing questions, encourage them to ask similar questions about other students' thinking. This supports them in further developing understandings. The Classroom-Tested Tip on page 16 provides additional information about probing questions. In addition, examples of how to implement this type of questioning are modeled in the student dialogues throughout the book.

Group Work

Provide daily opportunities for students to work in pairs, trios, or small groups to solve and discuss problems. Prekindergarten students are able to work in pairs, while students in kindergarten through grade 2 are capable of working together in smaller groups as well as in pairs. Use both homogeneous and heterogeneous groups when planning small-group work within a large-group lesson. Group work allows students to informally discuss problems together in a less threatening environment and to compare their ideas with their classmates' ideas. Mathematical language is modeled by students' peers in their small-group discussions, and they will be sharing the various strategies they use to solve problems. We can utilize this time to observe what is happening mathematically in the groups. It is a time to consider such questions as:

- What strategies are students using?

- How are students thinking about the mathematics in the activity?

- What are different students' roles in the problem-solving activity?

When students are working in groups, encourage them to solicit your help. Your role is that of a facilitator who guides students as they collaboratively solve mathematical tasks.

Models, Manipulatives, and Technological Tools

Working with materials in multiple representations strengthens students' understanding of the mathematics they are learning and provides a context for many abstract ideas. These tools help students to think through a problematic situation, to prove their conjectures in a concrete or pictorial way, and to communicate their reasoning about a concept. In the beginning of the school year, introduce students to the manipulatives they will be using throughout the year so that they will be familiar with the materials and the vocabulary associated with them. Provide students with easy access to these manipulatives and expect them to assume responsibility of the materials they are using daily.

CLASSROOM-TESTED TIP

The models and manipulatives that students utilize to represent their problem solving and reasoning become powerful tools in their mathematical development. When students use mathematical representations to interact with mathematics, it helps them to reason by analogy. "These concrete and pictorial aids are analogies of the mathematical ideas. That is, they are designed to mirror the structure of an abstract concept. The analogues serve as a tangible source from which the child can construct a mental model of the mathematical concept" (Stiff 1999, 23).

It is therefore important that the materials, or analogues, we provide students clearly support them to make sense of the mathematical concept being represented. We will be strengthening our students' ability to reason by analogy, which is a beneficial tool in problem solving and in posing problems.

Technology can also be used as a tool to enrich students' learning, and problem-solving programs have been developed that encourage students' use of spatial reasoning, in addition to other types of reasoning. Several websites have been recommended for your students' use in the section titled "Resources to Support Teachers" near the end of this book. Although the use of models and manipulatives is critical in students' mathematics learning, it should not be the only means of instruction. These representations serve as a bridge to help students connect to and make sense of more abstract mathematical thinking. The conversations they have with you and other students about their representations will further clarify how they are thinking and reasoning about a concept or skill. In Chapter 5, the value of representation will be discussed in more detail.

Reflecting on Problem Solving and Reasoning

As part of your classroom expectations, encourage all students to reflect on any mathematics they are learning about, especially how they are thinking about a problem, the strategies they are using to solve it, and its solution. Young students can learn to ask themselves, "Is my answer right?" This helps students to self-monitor their own thinking, and it allows them an opportunity to revise reasoning if necessary. A supportive and collaborative classroom environment promotes this reflective thinking. For very young children, begin by asking them to reflect in a small group setting. The skills learned here can be used in larger group discussions later.

High Standards and Expectations

Students have a right to be challenged and to make sense of the mathematics they are learning. "All students, regardless of their personal characteristics, backgrounds, or physical challenges, must have opportunities to study—and support to learn—mathematics" (NCTM 2000, 12). Every student should have daily opportunities to participate in experiences that involve reasoning about mathematics.

Final Thoughts

As you reflect on this chapter, remember to set reasonable expectations when you begin transitioning to a learning culture that promotes reasoning. The establishment of a positive climate is the most critical factor in creating this environment, which will benefit all students. We must clearly convey to students that we value their ways of reasoning and that we also expect them to respect and value each other's thinking and reasoning. We must also let students know that mathematics should make sense to them so that learning becomes meaningful.

Make it a priority to help your students understand that they will be expected to communicate their thinking and reasoning in a variety of ways. As teachers we often reflect on our own learning, and we must expect our students to do the same. When we provide students time to think about their reasoning, refinements can be made that support them in communicating more clearly about their reasoning.

Another important goal to consider is ensuring the equity of educational opportunities for all of our students. All students must be encouraged and supported as they begin to develop and use reasoning skills. Just as our students' conceptual understanding and skills are at different levels, their reasoning abilities will be, too. Many of the "Classroom-Tested Tip" boxes throughout the chapters provide suggestions that will help you manage the diversity of your students' learning needs.

Although the goal of becoming a reasoning classroom may not be accomplished quickly, the journey is a worthwhile one. Providing your students with ongoing opportunities to reason about important mathematical ideas and relationships begins to develop flexible habits of mind. Helping students to become powerful thinkers who reason thoughtfully and make sense of what they are learning will certainly prepare them for higher learning and their future roles in life.

Questions for Discussion

1. How do you personally feel about mathematics? How will your feelings affect your students' learning of mathematics?

2. Think about how your students will feel about being more actively involved in learning mathematics. What will you do to make this transition easier?

3. Which of the factors that help promote reasoning are you already implementing in your teaching of mathematics? How well are they working? Will you change them in any way?

4. Which, if any, factors will be difficult for you to begin implementing into your daily teaching? Why do you think this is the case? Talk with colleagues about strategies that will make it more manageable for you to implement these factors.

CHAPTER 2

Reasoning in Prekindergarten Through Grade 2

Mathematics is a discipline that deals with abstract entities, and reasoning is the tool for understanding abstraction.

—Lee Stiff, *Developing Mathematical Reasoning in Grades K–12*

What Can You Expect of Students?

Before grade 3, students' reasoning is based mostly on the knowledge that something is right because it has happened before. Young students reason that because their teacher, a family member, or another adult told them it was so, then it has to be true. Finally, if students have seen something happen a certain way several times before, they think it must always happen in that way. Therefore, we must be persistent in expecting students to explain their thinking in our daily mathematics discussions.

"Being able to explain one's thinking by stating reasons is an important skill for formal reasoning that begins at this level" (NCTM 2000, 123). When we consistently expect primary students to explain their reasoning, it lays the foundation for making informal justifications. This beginning development of reasoning should become a strong focus for all mathematics learning at these grade levels. Encourage students to give examples for why something is true or why it is correct. This strengthens students' abilities to justify or disprove conjectures with mathematical arguments. By the end of grade 2, students are finding that counterexamples can disprove reasoning.

Primary students naturally reason in a variety of daily experiences. Children's early reasoning helps them make sense of their immediate surroundings. Their reasoning is mainly intuitive, and they often do not think of reasoning as a way to solve a problem. But it is vital that we support our students in their efforts to explain their thinking and provide justifications for this early reasoning.

Before entering grade 3, many primary students' justifications involve only examples. Some students in grades 1 and 2 are beginning to reason beyond a single object or example to generalizing among classes of objects or examples (e.g., conjecturing about number relationships such as odd and even numbers). Here are several questions that encourage students to make generalizations:

■ Will this work with other numbers?

■ What do you think will happen if you solve more problems this way?

■ Do you think this strategy will work every time?

Exploring a mathematical idea more thoroughly will allow students the opportunity to refine and strengthen their reasoning about it.

CLASSROOM-TESTED TIP

Daily Routines

Establishing daily routines is a powerful way to support students' developing reasoning skills. Routines such as calendar math, number of the day, or "Guess My Number" strengthen children's number concepts, illustrate number relationships, and build number sense. Young students' ability to think about numbers in different ways helps them reason with numbers in complex ways. Our implementation of daily routines is critical because these routines provide students with opportunities to engage in meaningful mathematical discussions that help them make sense of the math they are learning. For example, in a number of the day routine, teachers might focus on the day's date and ask students to describe what they know about that number. Following are examples of what students might say on the fifteenth day of the month.

1 more than 14	5 more than 10
1 more than double 7	half of 30
an odd number	a dime and a nickel
my brother's age	number of kids in our class
1 less than 16	the third number you say when you count by 5's (5, 10, 15)

Describing numbers in a variety of ways allows students to use mathematical language to describe relationships among numbers. These experiences support students' ability to reason more thoughtfully about number relationships.

We can support young children's ability to reason and construct understanding of mathematics concepts by establishing an ongoing calendar mathematics routine. This daily routine benefits children's mathematical learning in these ways: (1) students connect mathematics to their everyday lives, (2) students' number sense is strengthened, (3) students have daily opportunities to share observations and to describe a variety of problem-solving strategies, (4) students' oral language skills and mathematics vocabulary are supported, and (5) teachers are provided with informal assessment information about students' conceptual understanding and skill development as they listen to students explaining their thinking. Following are several examples of calendar activities:

■ **Representing the dates on a calendar grid in a pattern.** Students will use inductive thinking to predict a teacher's chosen pattern as date cards are added one day at a time. The end of the month is an opportune time for students to notice additional visual patterns on this monthly grid.

■ **Recording students' birthdays in a graphic format or collecting data about the number of days a type of weather has occurred during the month.** Ongoing discussions reinforce students' understandings about number operations, number relationships (e.g., more than, less than, and same as), and reasoning about the data displayed on the graph. In Chapter 5, a kindergarten student dialogue is presented to demonstrate this component of a calendar routine.

■ **Keeping track of the days students have been in school on a roll of adding machine tape that is displayed in the classroom.** For example, a grade 2 teacher might record the days as they occur in the following pattern: odd numbers in black and even numbers in red, every fifth day circled in green, and every tenth day with a purple square drawn around it. This routine reinforces number sense; counting strategies such as counting on and back; addition and subtraction; before, after, between; visual patterns; multiples of 2's, 5's, and 10's. It also supports students' thinking and reasoning skills as they answer questions about the number line that is forming throughout the school year.

Another daily routine is a game called "Guess My Number." In this chapter, a grade 2 student dialogue demonstrates how you can use this simple routine to help students build their reasoning skills.

Types of Reasoning

One of the most commonly used types of reasoning is actually quite simple. It involves reasoning from an intuition, or having a feeling about something. Students often rely on intuition when they have limited information. Decisions based on intuitive reasoning can often be correct, but because of the limits of intuitive reasoning, many of these decisions are incorrect (Baroody 1993). Despite its limitations, this type of reasoning is helpful for students when they are solving problems and therefore should be encouraged; however, it is crucial that we expect students to support intuitive reasoning with examples. Our facilitation of student discussions and the probing questions we ask will help students reflect on their thinking so that they can better describe their reasoning.

Inductive and deductive reasoning, as well as intuitive reasoning, are useful in mathematics and students' everyday lives. In inductive reasoning, students' thinking proceeds from specific ideas or examples to a generality or a pattern. Important opportunities for students to reason inductively are experiences in which they are able to recognize, extend, and generalize patterns as well as write rules using words or symbols to describe these patterns. In deductive reasoning, students reach a specific conclusion based on what they know. Deduction involves students' ability to infer a new relationship from given information. Ideas and ways to implement inductive and deductive reasoning are provided for you in this chapter, including sample dialogues of students using both types of reasoning.

In Chapter 7, we discuss how students reason differently across the content standards. Examples of students using algebraic reasoning and spatial reasoning are demonstrated in the student dialogues of Chapter 7. Several of the student dialogues are discussions of activities included on the CD. The CD provides activities for each of the following content standards: number and operations, algebra, geometry, measurement, and data analysis and probability.

Inductive Reasoning

Patterns are the heart of mathematics, and inductive reasoning provides the vehicle for students to discover this. When students are reasoning inductively, they are exploring important mathematical ideas about patterns, relationships, and generalities. Patterning experiences should be provided for students throughout the elementary years. In prekindergarten through grade 2, students' work with patterns involves repeating and growing patterns. Patterning activities are powerful in supporting and developing students' inductive reasoning abilities (Figure 2–1).

In addition to patterning experiences, sorting and classifying activities are critical to students' development of thinking skills and inductive reasoning. Vocabulary such as *some, none, if, or, all*, and *not* are informally used by children as they describe how objects are sorted. Understanding this vocabulary helps students when they are reasoning about mathematics in more complex situations. Comparison circles provide students with a tool that organizes their thinking about the attributes they are noticing in the objects they are sorting. Noticing attributes of 2- and 3-dimensional figures, and observing how these shapes are alike and different, lead students to recognize that different shapes can also have similar attributes. For example, an important idea for students to reason about involves the classification of quadrilaterals. While squares, trapezoids, rectangles, parallelograms, and rhombi are different shapes to young children, we want them to also recognize that these shapes have two attributes in common: four vertices and four sides. Young students benefit from ongoing experiences that focus on shapes' attributes. These experiences strengthen students' inductive

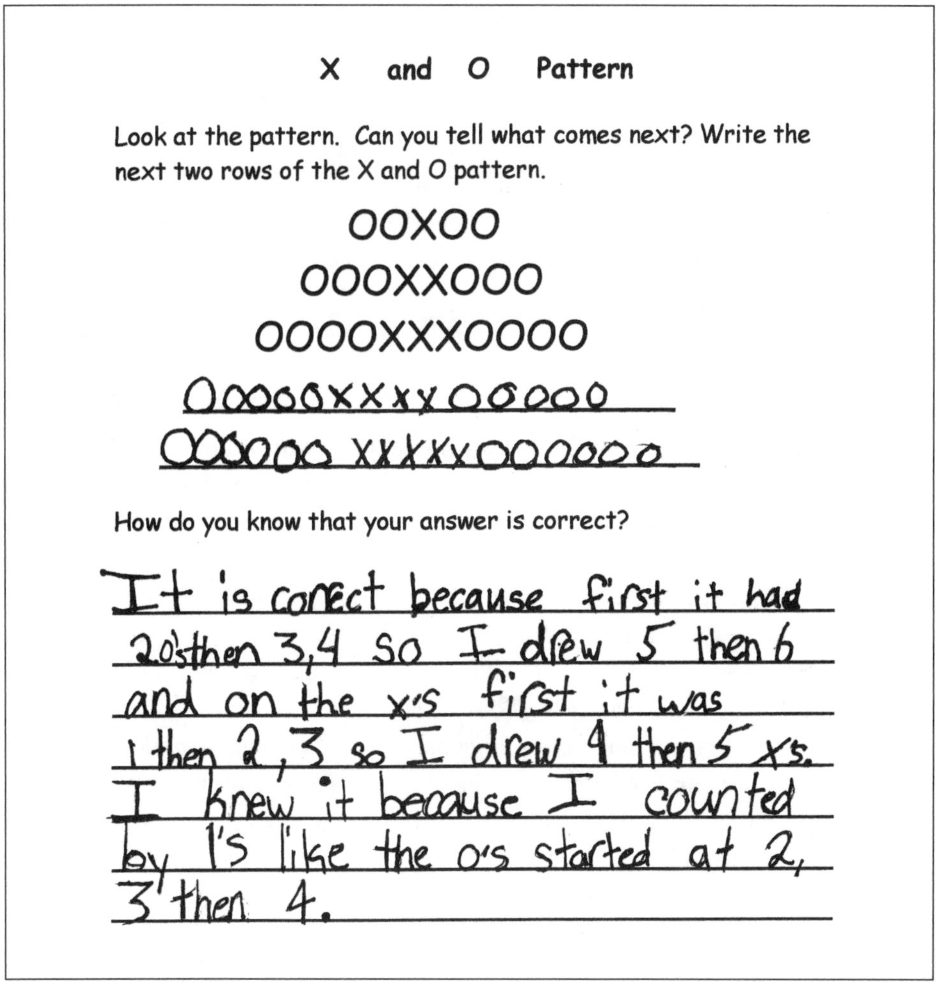

X and O Pattern

Look at the pattern. Can you tell what comes next? Write the next two rows of the X and O pattern.

OOXOO

OOOXXOOO

OOOOXXXOOOO

OOOOOXXXXOOOOO

OOOOOO XXXXXOOOOOO

How do you know that your answer is correct?

It is correct because first it had 2 o's then 3,4 so I drew 5 then 6 and on the x's first it was 1 then 2,3 so I drew 4 then 5 x's. I knew it because I counted by 1's like the o's started at 2, 3 then 4.

Figure 2–1 *A student's explanation for how a pattern is growing.*

reasoning skills and help them to develop foundational understandings necessary to reason and generalize about classes of shapes in later years.

When formulating conjectures, students are using inductive reasoning. We can help students to understand that before a statement or conjecture is considered a rule, or always true, it must be explained and tested with a variety of examples. We want students to also understand that just one counterexample will disprove a conjecture. Deductive reasoning then plays an important part in proving or disproving a conjecture.

Another activity that requires inductive thinking is a function machine (or function table), in which an input number is changed to an output value based on a specific rule. In many textbook lessons, students generally complete a function table based on an already identified rule that tells them how to fill in the missing input numbers or output values. However, if the task is changed by asking students to generate the rule of the function table based on several input and output examples, then they have the opportunity to explore inductive thinking more deeply. Function tables are generally a focus in the intermediate grades and beyond, but primary students are intrigued by function tables as well.

The following discussion occurred in a grade 2 classroom as the teacher introduced a function table as a "number machine."

TEACHER: This is a number machine. To use this machine, we can put any number into it. The machine first subtracts an amount from the number we put into it, and then it adds an amount. Finally, a new number comes out. I'm going to put a nine in the number machine. The machine subtracts two. What would you get if you subtract two from nine?

STUDENT: Seven.

TEACHER: Explain how you know that.

STUDENT: I just know that.

TEACHER: Explain how to get the answer if you don't "just know it."

STUDENT: *(Student thinks for a moment.)* Well, you just count back two times from nine. Start at nine and go back one time to eight, and the second time you're at seven.

TEACHER: Thank you for that explanation. Now the machine will add four to our new number, which is seven. What happens now?

STUDENT: It's eleven because seven and four is eleven. I know seven and three is ten and four is one more than three. So it's eleven.

TEACHER: So out of the number machine comes . . . *(All students respond, "Eleven.")* Let's put other numbers in the machine. I'm putting in a five now. What do you think the number will be that comes out of the machine at the other end?

STUDENT: I think seven will come out

TEACHER: Why do you think seven will be the final number?

STUDENT: If you minus two, that equals three. Then if you add four, that equals seven.

TEACHER: Does everyone agree? *(All agree.)*

TEACHER: OK, the next number I'll put into the machine is 52.

STUDENT: If you subtract two from 52, you get 50. Then add four and you get 54. And I think that's the answer.

The teacher placed several more numbers into the machine and solicited additional student responses and explanations. She recorded the students' responses in a table labeled *In* and *Out* (Figure 2–2). Her warm-up not only provided students with an opportunity to mentally subtract and add numbers, it also enabled them to become familiar with the number machine and the rules of the machine. Students' understanding of how the machine's rules of "subtract two" and "add four" affected the output value was important. In the next part of the lesson, students were given the opportunity to reason about the relationship between the input numbers and the output values.

TEACHER: Let's think about the number machine in a different way. So far we have been trying to figure out what number comes out of the machine using the rules on the machine. Now I'd like you to figure out what number went in at the beginning if ten is the number that came out.

STUDENT: Whoa! That's harder!

Figure 2–2 *These students are reviewing the results
of the number machine lesson.*

STUDENT: I think it's twelve.

TEACHER: Explain why you think that.

STUDENT: I think twelve because if you subtract two, you would make ten, and then
you add four.

TEACHER: What happens when you add four to ten?

STUDENT: *(thinks for several seconds)* Never mind. That won't work. That's more
than ten.

TEACHER: So you're saying twelve is not our number that went in at the beginning?
(Student agrees.) Does everyone else agree? *(All agree.)* Talk with someone near
you about the number you think went into the machine. Remember ten is the number that came out of the machine. Think about the rules of the machine. *(Teacher
points to the number machine on the blackboard.)*

Students were given several minutes to discuss this problem with each other. As
students were problem solving together, the teacher observed several pairs of students
to listen to their reasoning about the problem. She was gathering informal information
about how the students were thinking about the problem.

TEACHER: All right, you've had time to talk about what number could have gone into the machine if the final number was ten. Our rules for the number machine are to first subtract two and then add four. Who would like to share what you and your partner were discussing?

STUDENT: We think it's six.

TEACHER: Tell us more about how you and your partner decided it was six.

STUDENT: Well, six plus two equals eight. *(Teacher notices that many students are visually disagreeing and decides to allow for clarification of the rules of the number machine.)*

SECOND STUDENT: We disagree because the first thing the machine does is to subtract two and then it adds four.

TEACHER: What do you think? *(to student who began explaining)*

STUDENT: Oh, yeah. That's right. Subtract two from six and that gives you four. Then add four and that gives you eight. Wait, that doesn't make ten.

TEACHER: Would you like more time to think about what number went into the machine at the beginning? *(The student pair is given time to think.)* OK, we know twelve and six will not make the machine end with ten. *(Teacher records these two numbers on the board so that students have a record of their work so far in solving this task.)* Talk with your partner again for a minute. Discuss whether the number you chose works with the rules on the number machine.

This brief time for students to talk again provided the original student pair (with the incorrect response of "six") additional stress-free wait time because everyone was discussing the problem in their pair groupings. The teacher then called on the original pair to share their revised thinking and reasoning.

STUDENT: We think it's eight now.

TEACHER: How do you know?

STUDENT: You put in an eight, the eight turns into a six, and then you add four to the six, and you get ten!

TEACHER: Does *(student's)* answer make sense to all of you? *(Students agree.)* Let's record this work on our chart. *(Teacher records "eight" on the table already begun during the first part of the lesson.)*

The teacher presented several more "end" numbers and asked students to predict what numbers went into the number machine. These numbers were then recorded on the table.

TEACHER: We've been recording the numbers that went into the number machine and the numbers that went out after the rules have been completed. What do you notice about the numbers in the *In* and *Out* columns? *(Teacher gives students think time.)*

STUDENT: We always have a higher number in the *Out* column.

TEACHER: Thank you. Did anyone notice something different?

STUDENT: It goes in 9 and comes out 11. It goes 9, 11; 5, 7; 52, 54. It's changing by two every time.

TEACHER: Tell us what you mean when you say, "changing by two."

STUDENT: Well, from start to end the numbers changed by two. They got bigger by two.

TEACHER: If I put in eleven what is going to come out?

STUDENT: Thirteen, because eleven minus two equals nine and nine plus four equals thirteen!

TEACHER: If eight came out, what went in?

STUDENT: Six. Six minus two equals four. Four plus four equals eight.

TEACHER: So do we have a pattern on the *In* and *Out* columns of "plus two?"

STUDENT: Sorta. We really had two rules first. Subtract two and then add four.

TEACHER: I see. And when we followed those rules what happened between the *In* and *Out* columns?

STUDENT: Each time the number got bigger by two.

Students were learning to reason inductively by completing a function machine with the rules known. The supportive environment established by this teacher encouraged students to take risks that allowed them to refine and edit statements about the answers being discussed. Although students were not generalizing or conjecturing about the rules on the "number machine," they were noticing a pattern that could be generalized and then making a statement about the relationship between the input numbers and the output values. When the teacher recorded information on a chart, students were able to notice that in each pair, the output value was always larger than the input number by two. Once they understood the relationship between the input number and the output value, students were able to predict the input number quickly based on the output value or vice versa. Students were then expected to check their predictions against the rules of the number machine. This type of activity allows students to explore the relationship between the input numbers and output values on an informal function machine table (Figure 2–3).

CLASSROOM-TESTED TIP

Make it a priority to always ask "How do you know?" when students respond to a question, whether their answer is correct or incorrect. This gives students an opportunity to reflect on their response. If the answer is correct, others will benefit from the student's explanation of how he arrived at the answer, what strategy he used, and why the solution makes sense. If the answer is incorrect, the student has an opportunity to revise and edit any errors in his problem solving and reasoning, and other students will also have an opportunity to think about and analyze the errors. We often correct our students' errors before they can reflect on them. Students should see that errors are valuable learning experiences. *It is essential that we allow our students multiple opportunities to analyze errors in problem solving and reasoning.* This will help them deepen the important understandings of the mathematics they are learning.

Melissa's Age

Melissa puts her age in this In- Out Machine.
The number that comes out is her sister's age.

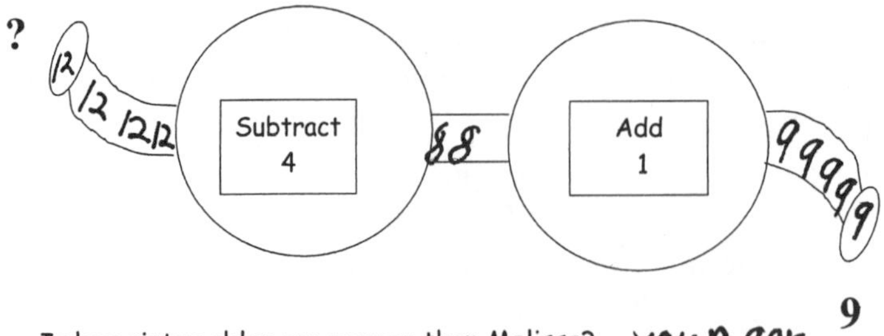

Is her sister older or younger than Melissa? __younger__

Explain your thinking.

I put in 12 subtracted 4 and 8
came out and then I added 1 to
8 wich makes 9.

In 2 years if Melissa puts in her age, what will her sister's age be? _11_

Explain your thinking.

In two years Mellissa will be
14 wich means her sister will
be 11.

Figure 2–3 *This CD activity was completed by a student as an extension of the number machine lesson.*

Deductive Reasoning

Students use deductive reasoning when testing conjectures that have resulted from inductive reasoning. Children also use deductive reasoning in everyday problem solving. To help students develop deductive reasoning, provide experiences in which they are solving complex word problems as well as logical-thinking problems. These kinds of problems differ from traditional word problems because they contain constraints that increase the complexity of the problems. Following is an example of this type of problem:

Nicholas has forty cents in his pocket. He does not have any pennies. What coins could he have in his pocket?

In solving the problem, it is necessary for students to consider two constraints. The first constraint limits the amount of money Nicholas has, and the second constraint is that there are no pennies. Because of the number of coin combinations possible, students will soon discover that they need to organize their thinking to make sense of the problem based on the constraints presented. Logical-thinking problems involve more constraints than traditional word problems. Students are given information, or clue statements, to help them eliminate possible solutions in order to answer the question. Students can use various organizing tools to help them make sense of the problem.

Another type of problem that causes students to think logically is one in which students must provide the "clues" or ask the questions that narrow the choices to a specific answer. The students in this grade 1 classroom were using a 100-chart to solve the challenge that was presented. A 100-chart was on the overhead projector, and the teacher had chosen a student to be in charge of organizing the information the students gathered based on the questions asked. Following is the discussion:

TEACHER: We're going to play a game called "Guess My Number." You have eight guesses to figure out what the mystery number is. You cannot ask if it is a specific number. "Is it 65?" is not an acceptable question. Does everyone understand this rule? *(Students indicate understanding.)* The mystery number is between 1 and 100. Talk at your table about questions that would be helpful in figuring out the mystery number. *(Students discuss possible questions for about a minute.)* Who would like to ask the first question?

STUDENT: Is it higher or lower than 15?

TEACHER: The mystery number is greater than 15. What numbers can it not be?

STUDENT: It can't be any numbers lower than 15 like 14 and on down. *(Student crosses out numbers 1 through 14 on 100-chart.)*

TEACHER: Could it be 15?

STUDENT: *(Student is given wait time.)* No, because you said the number was greater than 15 so we have to cross out 15, too.

TEACHER: That's your first guess. We have seven guesses left. Who has another question?

STUDENT: Is it greater than 25?

TEACHER: The mystery number is greater than 25. What numbers can we cross off now?

STUDENT: All the numbers between 15 and 26. *(Teacher crosses off all numbers from 16 through 25.)*

TEACHER: *(to another student)* Explain what numbers *(original student)* means.

STUDENT: I think she's saying to cross off 25 first because you said the number is greater than 25. Then you cross off all the numbers down to 16 because the numbers 1 to 15 are already crossed off.

TEACHER: So what do we know after two guesses?

STUDENT: That the mystery number is greater than 25!

STUDENT: Is it greater than 35?

TEACHER: Yes. It is greater than 35. What numbers can it not be?

STUDENT: We can cross out 26 all the way up to 35 now. Do 35 because you said the number is more than 35.

TEACHER: That's three questions.

STUDENT: Is it greater than 45?

TEACHER: Yes. It is greater than 45. *(Student crosses out numbers.)*

STUDENT: Is it greater than 52?

TEACHER: Yes, it is greater than 52. All right, how many guesses do we have left? We've done 5.

STUDENT: Three!

TEACHER: How do you know we have three guesses left?

STUDENT: Because five and three more is eight.

STUDENT: Is it greater than 62?

TEACHER: It is greater than 62. *(Numbers are crossed out.)* All right, that was the sixth question. You have two questions left. What numbers could it be?

STUDENT: It could be any number from 63 up to 100.

STUDENT: I disagree. You said it was between 1 and 100. I think that means it can't be 100.

TEACHER: What do the rest of you think about 100? What does the word *between* mean? *(The discussion continues after an explanation is given.)* Think of a question that gives you lots of information. Remember there are only two questions left.

STUDENT: Is it greater than 70?

TEACHER: It is not greater than 70. What do we record on the 100-chart?

STUDENT: You can cross out all the numbers above 70.

TEACHER: You have one question left. What numbers could it be?

STUDENT: It could be 63, 64, 65, 66, 67, 68, 69, or 70.

STUDENT: Is it greater than 65?

TEACHER: Let's think about this question. This is the last question. Is there a question that gives us more information about the mystery number? *(Students are given wait time.)*

STUDENT: Is it greater than 66?

TEACHER: It is not greater than 66. That was your last question. The mystery number is 64. I see you are disappointed that you didn't figure out the mystery number. Think of what you know about numbers and talk again at your table to think of new questions that might be more helpful in our next game. *(Students brainstorm questions for several minutes.)*

STUDENT: We could ask if the number is between two numbers.

TEACHER: Explain how asking that gives us more information.

STUDENT: If it is between two numbers, we can cross off all the numbers below and above the numbers.

TEACHER: *(Student),* would you give us an example of what she means?

STUDENT: I think she means if the number is between 30 and 70, all the numbers from 30 down to 1 won't work, and all the numbers from 70 to 100 won't work either. That got rid of a bunch of numbers.

STUDENT: Ask if the number is odd or even. That helps a lot!

TEACHER: Why do you think so?

STUDENT: Because half of numbers are odd and half are even. That's because one is odd, two is even and you keep going. Odd, even, odd, even!

TEACHER: Is there anything else we know about numbers?

STUDENT: You ask if the number has one or two numbers in it?

TEACHER: What do you mean?

STUDENT: Eight has one number in it, and 52 has two numbers in it.

TEACHER: So you're saying a one-digit number would be eight and a two-digit number would be 52. Is that what you said? *(Student agrees.)*

TEACHER: Let's try a different mystery number. This time you have six guesses.

STUDENT: Is it an odd number?

TEACHER: It is not an odd number. What numbers could it not be?

STUDENT: You have to cross out the whole column under the one, the three, the five, the seven, and the nine. *(See Figure 2–4.)*

TEACHER: How do you know?

STUDENT: Those are all odd numbers.

TEACHER: That eliminated a lot of numbers! So you found out one question can give you a lot of information. How many numbers are now eliminated?

STUDENT: Fifty numbers, because there are five columns of numbers, and there are ten numbers in each column. You count 10, 20, 30, 40, 50.

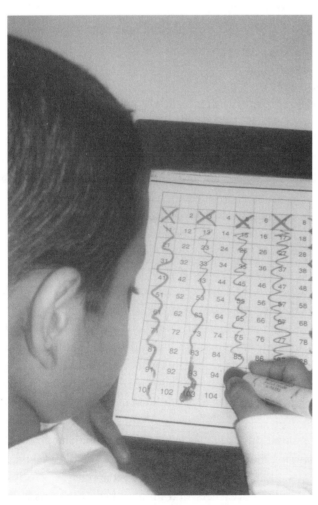

Figure 2–4 *A student eliminates all the odd numbers in a Guess My Number activity.*

TEACHER: That was your first question.

STUDENT: Is it a one-digit number?

TEACHER: It is not a one-digit number. So which numbers do we eliminate? *(Students say 2, 4, 6, and 8.)*

STUDENT: Is it between 44 and 50?

TEACHER: There are only two even numbers between 44 and 50. Think about a question that eliminates more numbers. *(Student is given wait time.)*

STUDENT: Ok, is it between 55 and 99?

TEACHER: Yes, it is between 55 and 99. What numbers can we eliminate now? *(Students say all even numbers from 54 and below and 100.)* So we know the mystery number is an even number between 55 and 99. That was our third question.

STUDENT: Is it bigger than 80?

TEACHER: Yes, the mystery number is greater than 80. *(Students eliminate all even numbers from 80 and below.)* You have two guesses left. What number could it be? Look at the chart to help you think about the possible answers.

STUDENT: It has to be an even number from 82 to 98 because we know it's not 80 or 100.

STUDENT: Is it between 90 and 100?

TEACHER: Yes, it is between 90 and 100. That was the fifth question. What numbers could it be?

STUDENT: It can be 92, 94, 96, or 98.

STUDENT: Does it have a six in the ones place?

TEACHER: Wow! Yes, it has a six in the ones place. So the mystery number is. . . . ?

CLASS: 96!

Students were learning to use a 100-chart to help them reason deductively in an organized manner. Without this tool, solving this problem may have been a confusing and frustrating experience for students. The teacher's facilitation of the student discussion enabled students to reason deductively in an environment that encouraged risk taking. In the beginning, the students asked very specific questions. When the teacher observed that students' questions were eliminating few possibilities, she skillfully facilitated the discussion by asking students to discuss with one another what they knew about "numbers." This helped them to realize that by asking broader questions, many numbers could be eliminated. This strategy led them to the chosen number in a more efficient manner. In experiences such as "Guess My Number," students begin to understand that eliminating possibilities is important in logically thinking about a problem. With more experiences of this kind, these students will be able to independently solve similar complex problems and strengthen their ability to reason deductively. This type of reasoning is important because it is the thinking used in developing and justifying mathematical arguments.

Providing students with multiple opportunities to solve logical-thinking problems helps them to develop the thinking that is foundational for more complicated types of reasoning in later school years. Number logic problems are yet another way to support your students' reasoning abilities. Teachers find number logic problems to be both motivating and engaging for students to solve, and they also strengthen students' number sense abilities.

In the process of discussing and solving this problem students were:

- strengthening number sense;

- working on a challenging problem;

- describing relationships among numbers;

- using deductive reasoning skills; and

- discussing an engaging problem that produced rich talk about the targeted mathematics.

Additional Tools That Support Students' Reasoning Skills

Teachers find that games are highly motivating for students. Mathematics games help students develop number sense and encourage them to think about and then use multiple strategies as they are playing. When students first play a game, their focus tends to be more on the rules of the game as they participate. However, once they are comfortable with the game's rules, students then begin to focus more on strategies and reasoning to play the game. By observing students as they are playing games, we can learn important information about their reasoning abilities. Give yourself time to observe and ask questions of your students as they are playing math games with classmates. In addition, the discussions you have with students following any game playing are critical and beneficial for your students as they develop the skills necessary for reasoning.

Another example of problem solving that involves logical thinking is magic squares. Magic squares are puzzles that require students to use both inductive and deductive reasoning in order to solve them. In the primary grade levels, they are generally formatted into a four-by-four or a three-by-three grid with some numbers missing on the grid. Students fill in the missing numbers so that all the columns, rows, and diagonals generate the same sum.

Inductive and Deductive Thinking in a Kindergarten Classroom

Near the beginning of this chapter, we briefly discussed the importance of providing students with opportunities to work with patterns to help develop inductive thinking. Early patterning experiences ask students to either extend a pattern or predict what comes next in a pattern. Young students benefit from "reading" patterns (e.g., red, green, red, green, red, green, . . .) These experiences help students to develop their thinking about the part, or unit, of the pattern that repeats and eventually enables them to predict what appears later in a pattern sequence. Understanding which elements repeat or how elements in a particular pattern are related is a big idea that is difficult for very young learners. We can deepen our students' understanding of patterns by

---

Lunch

Peggy, William, and Charles eat different lunches at school.
The lunches are a pizza, a peanut butter and jelly sandwich, and
a taco.

Read the clues to find out what each student eats.

- ○ William did not have pizza or a taco.
- ○ Charles did not have a taco.

William eats <u>Peanut butter and Jelly.</u>

Peggy eats <u>tacos</u>.

Charles eats <u>Pizza</u>.

How do you know your answer is correct?

<u>It is correct because William did not</u>
<u>have pizza or tacos Charles did not have</u>
<u>tacos and Peggt can't eat peanut</u>
<u>butter and jelly because somwon hase gnote</u>
<u>tok it and it can't be pizza because</u>
<u>it hase ban tacon.</u>

Figure 2–5 *A student's response to a logical thinking task from the CD.*

asking them to tell what part of the pattern repeats. Asking students to break a pattern apart by its repeating units is also beneficial. For example, when students break apart a stick of twelve connecting cubes that have been made into an AB pattern of red and blue cubes, they concretely see the parts, or units, that make up this pattern.

Following is a kindergarten dialogue in which students were predicting parts of a pattern that were hidden.* The lesson challenged students to think both inductively and deductively by focusing on the elements of the repeating pattern. Students were first asked to describe several patterns shown by the teacher (AB, ABC, and AAB patterns). In addition, she asked them to describe the part of each pattern that repeated. Then the teacher introduced the game, "What Do You Think?"

---

*This lesson was adapted from the work of Carole E. Greenes, Linda Dacey, Mary Cavanagh, Carol R. Findell, Linda Jensen Sheffield, and Marian Small in *Navigating through Problem Solving and Reasoning in Prekindergarten—Kindergarten* (2003, 14–16).

TEACHER: We will be playing a game called "What Do You Think?" *(The teacher had previously made a simple AB pattern and covered each element of the pattern with a cut-out window.)* Behind every window is an orange square or a yellow hexagon. I want you to figure out which shape is behind each window. *(Teacher calls on a student to open a window.)*

STUDENT: *(opening the second window)* It's a square.

TEACHER: How do you know it's a square?

STUDENT: All its sides are the same.

TEACHER: Does anyone know something else about a square?

STUDENT: It has four pointy parts. *(Student points to the four corners, or vertices.)*

TEACHER: *(to all students)* Think about the shape you just saw. Tell a friend what shape you think is behind the third door and tell why you think this.

TEACHER: *(Student)*, please share what you think the next shape will be.

STUDENT: I think another shape is next, but I don't know what it is.

STUDENT: I know. It's a yellow one.

TEACHER: Explain why you think that.

STUDENT: I use the yellow one a lot, and it could be a yellow one and a square one and then a yellow one here.

TEACHER: So you are saying that a yellow hexagon will come after the orange square. If you agree with *(the student's)* prediction, tell a friend why. If you do not agree with the prediction, tell your friend what shape you think will be next.

TEACHER: *(Student)*, do you agree with *(original student)* that there will be a yellow hexagon here? *(pointing to window after the uncovered orange square)*

STUDENT: Yes.

TEACHER: Explain why you think it's a yellow hexagon.

STUDENT: It's a pattern that is yellow, square, yellow, square.

TEACHER: *(revealing a yellow hexagon under the third window)* We can now see the second and third shape in this pattern. Under the second window is an orange square and under the third window is a yellow hexagon. What shape do you think is under the first window?

STUDENT: It's a hexagon!

TEACHERS: Do you all agree with *(student's)* prediction? *(All agree.)* How do you think he knew the first shape is a hexagon?

STUDENT: The first one is different than the second one to make the pattern.

TEACHER: Oh, I see. So in our pattern we have a hexagon, square, hexagon so far. What shape do you think is behind the fifth window in our pattern? Tell a friend why you think this.

STUDENT: It's a yellow shape because it's a pattern.

TEACHER: Can someone else explain why the yellow shape would be under the fifth window? This is tricky because we didn't look under the fourth window. How do we know for sure?

STUDENT: She's right. It goes yellow, orange, yellow, orange, yellow!

TEACHER: What part keeps repeating in the pattern? What do you think?

STUDENT: It does yellow and orange over and over and over!

TEACHER: So yellow hexagon and orange square repeats? *(Students agree.)*

TEACHER: Let's try another set of windows. These windows have squares and triangles behind them. Close your eyes while I hide the shapes behind the windows. *(Teacher arranges an AAB pattern that consists of triangle, triangle, square.)* This time I'm going to open the third window. What shape is behind it?

STUDENT: It's a square again!

TEACHER: All right, let's open another window. *(Teacher calls on student.)*

STUDENT: *(after opening the first window)* It's a triangle.

TEACHER: Are you sure that's a triangle?

STUDENT: Triangles have three sides and three points like this one.

TEACHER: What do you all think? Is a square or a triangle next? *(behind the second window)*

STUDENT: It isn't square, triangle, square, triangle.

TEACHER: I'm not sure I understand what you mean.

STUDENT: If the pattern was square, triangle, and square again there would be a square in the first window. But there's a triangle there.

STUDENT: Oh yeah, the pattern is different. That was a *(student claps hands once and taps legs once)* pattern. The square would be second if it was like the first one.

TEACHER: How do you know this pattern is different?

STUDENT: The second shape has to be different from the triangle. And the third shape would be another triangle. It isn't. See, the third shape is a square.

TEACHER: Let's leave the second shape covered for now. I'll show you the shapes behind the fourth and fifth windows *(triangle, triangle)*. Think about the shapes you see. Now tell a friend what shape you think is under the second window. *(Students talk for a minute.)*

STUDENT: I think it's a triangle.

TEACHER: Who else thinks that the second shape is a triangle? Tell us why.

STUDENT: It is a triangle because it's a triangle, triangle, square pattern.

TEACHER: You are thinking that a triangle is under the second window. Say the pattern to check your thinking. *(Several students read the pattern: "triangle, triangle, square, triangle, triangle, square," etc. pointing to each element of the pattern.)*

TEACHER: *(Opens the second window to reveal a triangle. Several more windows are revealed so that students see the pattern in its entirety.)* What is the part in our pattern that repeats? *(Students indicate triangle, triangle, square.)* Which window helped you predict what shapes were in the pattern?

STUDENT: The first one tells you how to start.

STUDENT: I want to see three shapes.

TEACHER: Could the windows that help you be the fifth, sixth, and seventh? *(pointing to the fifth, sixth, and seventh windows in the pattern)*

STUDENT: That's OK, but I have to check the beginning, too.

STUDENT: I have to say the pattern. Sometimes I'm wrong.

TEACHER: Work with a learning buddy. One buddy will make a pattern with the pattern blocks and cover the pattern with the windows. The other buddy will choose a window to open. Before opening it, the buddy must predict what shape is under the window. When one buddy figures out the pattern, trade places and start over. (See Figure 2–6.)

Figure 2–6 *A kindergarten student is making predictions about a pattern.*

This experience helped students to focus on the elements that made up the structures of each pattern. Experiences such as this activity begin to develop the understandings necessary for students to be able to generalize and compare more complex patterns in later grades. This activity allowed students to reason inductively when they reflected on the part of the pattern that repeated and to reason deductively when they identified specific elements of the pattern based on the generalizations they were forming. Students were also representing patterns in various ways, an experience that will support them in making more sophisticated generalizations and comparisons of patterns in the intermediate grades. Important components of algebraic reasoning were beginning to be developed in this fun and engaging kindergarten lesson.

Final Thoughts

Student discussions are essential in any mathematics lesson you present to your students. Simply asking students to complete a problem-solving activity without providing them with an opportunity to discuss their problem solving and reasoning deprives students and teachers of a valuable learning experience!

Encourage your students to engage in the type of discussions in which they are held accountable for talk, rather than you. This allows students to see that their thinking is the focus of the discussion. As students begin to listen to each other, they will begin to add contributions as well. Students will be encouraged to explain their thinking when they know their contributions are valued. Students in a classroom climate that is safe, respectful, and supportive of learning in a collaborative manner are more willing to challenge others' reasoning, which is an important aspect in the development of reasoning skills.

Intuitive, inductive, and deductive reasoning are all important types of reasoning. The discussions we have with our students, as well as our expectations for students to write and represent their reasoning, can support them in developing their ability to reason. We must expect our students to explain their reasoning in thinking about a task, whether the solution is incorrect or correct. Asking, "How do you know?" is a valuable instructional move. Students should understand that incorrect responses are important to their learning and are beneficial in helping them refine their reasoning.

The varied questions modeled by teachers in the student dialogues of this chapter are examples of how to initiate more reflective discussion from your students. The questions helped students to reason using inductive and deductive thinking skills. Remembering a list of questions may be overwhelming to you when you begin to have daily discussions with your students. Choose a few questions to ask in your initial discussions. This will help you become comfortable with the questions, and students will be hearing the same questions being consistently modeled. Knowing that the questions will be asked routinely helps students become comfortable with math talk. Once you are familiar with these initial questions, add more questions to your repertoire. Not only are questions modeled for you throughout this book's dialogues, but they are also listed in some of the "Classroom-Tested Tip" boxes in Chapter 1.

Questions for Discussion

1. How are the three types of reasoning discussed in this chapter different? Which of these types of reasoning did you have the most opportunities to use during your own education in the primary grades? How do you think that affected your mathematics abilities in later school years?

2. Will it be challenging for you to support your students in using the types of reasoning discussed in this chapter? Why or why not?

3. Think about, or discuss with your colleagues, how you might enhance or begin to change your instruction to include more reasoning opportunities for your students. What experiences will you provide your students to help them strengthen their reasoning abilities?

CHAPTER 3

Is It Always True? Making Conjectures

A conjecture is a guess, inference, theory, or prediction based on untested
or unproven—and, hence, uncertain or incomplete—evidence.

—Arthur J. Baroody and Ronald T. Coslick,
Fostering Children's Mathematical Power

The Role of Conjectures in Reasoning and Proof

Primary students are beginning to think and reason about generalizations. Children's early experiences with patterning are foundational for this type of reasoning. Students' experiences with identifying characteristics of shapes help them make comparisons that will lead to more developed generalizations among classes of shapes in the intermediate school years. The thinking necessary for formulating conjectures is being developed by young students when they are asked to predict what will happen next in a problem-solving situation and why it is so. When students make conjectures about mathematical relationships, they examine these relationships more thoroughly. This examination in turn enables students to gain a deeper understanding of the mathematics being learned.

Making conjectures, whether based on intuitive or inductive thinking, is a critical component of reasoning. Make it a habit to ask students when appropriate, "Is this true?" or "Is it always true?" Asking these questions helps students learn to develop and justify conjectures that are based on broader generalizations. When students formulate conjectures, they need to know that these conjectures should be supported by explanations and justifications, which then become informal mathematical arguments. To validate conjectures, students must use deductive reasoning to develop their justifications. Expecting young children to think about why something is always true

43

supports their developing abilities to make mathematical arguments. Provide a variety of materials and tools to help students when they are investigating conjectures, such as manipulatives, calculators, and measuring tools (rulers, balances, etc.). It is important to also encourage students to represent these informal mathematical arguments pictorially and/or symbolically.

Before leaving the primary grades, students learn that just one counterexample can disprove a conjecture, an important milestone in reasoning. The understanding of this idea prompts students to examine their own reasoning more closely, as well as the reasoning of others. Instead of automatically accepting a conjecture as true, students will begin to reflect more carefully about a proposed conjecture to determine if it makes sense mathematically.

As students begin to reason more about the mathematics they are learning in your daily discussions, they will sometimes share reasoning that doesn't make sense or is flawed. Our natural reaction is to correct a student's flawed reasoning and continue on with the lesson, but we actually deny students a valuable learning opportunity when we do this. In a classroom that promotes reasoning, students' misconceptions and flawed reasoning are critical pieces of information about how our students are thinking about a mathematical idea or relationship. We want our students to understand that flaws in reasoning should be viewed as a natural part of the reasoning process.

At first it may be difficult for students to identify any flaws in their own reasoning; however, they often find it easier to explain flaws in someone else's reasoning. Communicate to students that their reasoning may be challenged, and that when this occurs, these misunderstandings and flaws are a necessary part of learning. They should also understand that flawed reasoning will be examined with the intent of learning from it. This experience provides students an opportunity to reflect, analyze, and rethink the proposed conjecture, and allows students to know what it is like to think through reasoning that does not work or make sense. The probing questions you ask will support students in reexamining reasoning that is being shared, and students should be encouraged to revise any flawed reasoning that is identified during a discussion. Students who are comfortable with rethinking about reasoning will be better prepared to self-monitor their own thinking when similar problem-solving situations arise in later school years.

By providing primary students with early opportunities to think about simpler generalizations in the mathematics they are learning, we will help them progress to a deeper understanding that conjectures must be justified with examples to prove their validity. In the intermediate grades, this understanding allows students to move beyond examples to broader generalizations that will then become part of their mathematical arguments.

In this chapter, we examine how to provide students with experiences that encourage reasoning about and making conjectures. The important mathematics relationships that we want our students to make conjectures about are included in this chapter, and we provide questions to ask your students that will assist them in thinking about their reasoning. These questions focus students' thinking, which helps them to communicate conjectures that make sense and clearly convey the meaning of the generalizations. Again, as in previous chapters, a student dialogue is included to model how this type of reasoning could look in your classroom. "Students must practice looking for relationships, making conjectures, testing their conjectures, and explaining and justifying the generalizations they make" (Stiff 1999, 10).

How Can You Help Your Students Make Conjectures?

In order for students to begin the process of making conjectures, it is critical that an accepting classroom environment has been established. We want our students to view the process of making and sharing conjectures as a risk-free and comfortable experience. When you are beginning to support students in making and stating conjectures, we recommend that you first revisit Chapter 1. The factors described in that chapter are those that promote a reasoning classroom and will certainly make this transition smoother for you and your students.

Students articulate conjectures in words when they begin to learn how to conjecture. Over time with multiple experiences, they find that symbols will more precisely express their conjectures. Students who have experienced limited opportunities to reason and then explain their reasoning may find it difficult to state a conjecture about a relationship they are observing. Our support becomes critical in guiding students' thinking about mathematical ideas, patterns, and relationships they are reasoning about, so that their conjectures become more precise and understandable. This ability evolves over time with repeated experiences.

The questions we ask of our students assist them in learning how to articulate conjectures, and these questions guide them to consider how to state conjectures that are more clearly understandable. Students must know that it is acceptable to have a conjecture questioned, clarified, revised, and tested. This process sends an important message to our students that their conjectures will be carefully examined and revised if necessary. Understanding this expectation helps students to become more comfortable when sharing a conjecture with their peers.

A strategy for introducing students to the reasoning involved in making a conjecture about a generalization is to show students a mathematical number sentence and simply ask, "Is this true?" In answering this question, students must examine a number sentence, or an equation, more closely. A simple equation can produce a powerful discussion. This is evident in the following student discussion from a second-grade classroom. The teacher was implementing the strategy just described in a student discussion. He wrote this number sentence on the board: $4 + 0 = 4$.

TEACHER: *(pointing to the equation on the board)* Is this true?
STUDENT: $4 + 0 = 4$ because zero is a number that if you add or subtract it doesn't do anything to the number. So it's true.
TEACHER: Is it always true? What about $10 + 0 = 10$?
STUDENT: It's still true because with $10 + 0$, the zero still doesn't do anything to the 10. *(Teacher asks for several more examples and records these on board.)*
TEACHER: So, you're saying if you have a zero in the number sentence, the number doesn't change when you add? *(Students nod yes.)* Let's record this on chart paper

so that we can remember this. Mathematicians call this statement a conjecture. What we write is our thinking about why this is always true.

With the students' help, the following conjecture was recorded:

When you add and there's a zero in the number sentence, you get the same answer.

TEACHER: *(wanting students to further explore this reasoning about the initial conjecture)* What about this number sentence? *(Teacher writes 70 + 1 = 70 on board.)* Is this true?

CLASS: NO!

TEACHER: Now I'm confused. Will someone explain why the zero didn't work the same way in this number sentence?

STUDENT: Well, the zero is different this time because it's in the 70. When you add one to 70, it's 71.

TEACHER: But I heard everyone say that when you have a zero in a number sentence, and you add, you get the same number. This has a zero, and we added but you say it's not true. Tell me why it doesn't work in this number sentence.

STUDENT: Because you have to add a one this time.

STUDENT: And because the zero isn't where it's supposed to be.

TEACHER: Explain what you mean. *(pointing to the zero in the 70)* The zero can't be here?

STUDENT: It can be there but it's not the same as in the other number sentences. *(pointing to the list on the board)* But if you add a zero to 70, then you have the same answer.

TEACHER: All right, someone tell me how to write the number sentence so it is a true statement.

STUDENT: 70 + 0 = 70

TEACHER: So if we showed our conjecture to another second-grade student, would they understand our thinking about this?

STUDENT: I think we say that any time you add zero to a number, you will always get the same number.

STUDENT: Write some of the number sentences, too. *(Teacher crosses out original conjecture, rewrites students' new conjecture, and lists five examples that had been contributed by students earlier.)*

TEACHER: Think about this. All the number sentences we have listed are examples for our conjectures. What happens if we record the zero first in the number sentence? *(records 0 + 4 on board)* Does our conjecture still make this a true number sentence?

STUDENT: It still equals 4.

TEACHER: What are other number sentences that show our conjecture still works with zero at the beginning? *(Students offer other examples.)*

STUDENT: You can put zero in front of the plus sign or after the plus sign. It doesn't matter where it is because it'll just do nothing to the other number, like 0 + 8 = 8 or 8 + 0 = 8. You get the same answer both times!

The students worked in pairs to think about additional examples of zero being in a different place in the number sentence. Several responses were:

■ 0 + 20 = 20; 20 + 0 = 20

■ 13 + 0 = 13; 0 + 13 = 13

■ 0 + 6 = 6; 6 + 0 = 6

■ 145 + 0 = 145; 0 + 145 = 145

TEACHER: *(rereading the revised conjecture)* We found out it doesn't matter whether the zero is before or after the plus sign in the number sentence when adding. How can we rewrite our conjecture so it says exactly what we know about the addition of zero? Let's write our conjecture so that it is very clear.

After a brief discussion, students suggested the following revised conjecture:

When you add a zero before or after the plus sign to another number, you will still get the same number. (See Figure 3–1.)

This discussion would not have occurred if students had simply been asked, "What is four plus zero?" This type of question requires only a one-word answer; however, the teacher asked instead the question, "Is this true?" followed by "Is it always true?" These questions initiated a rich discussion about the identity property of addition. The teacher purposefully chose a number sentence and property of number that students were familiar with; therefore, when students considered a conjecture to

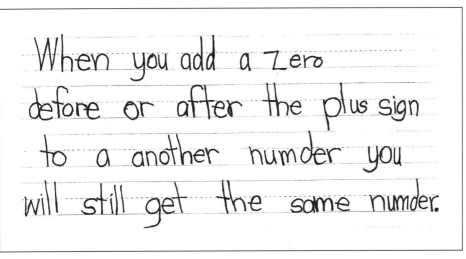

Figure 3–1 *A student's recording of the class-generated conjecture for the identity property of addition.*

describe why the number sentence was true, it was not an intimidating task for them. Students should not be expected to reason about mathematical ideas and relationships they know little about.

CLASSROOM-TESTED TIP

Record conjectures made by students on chart paper. Display these conjectures in a highly visible area in the classroom. As thinking about a conjecture changes because of students' developing mathematical understandings, allow them time to revisit and refine any conjectures previously recorded.

In examining the number sentence 4 + 0 = 4 closely, students were also able to state an informal generalization about the relationship they saw in 4 + 0 = 4 and 0 + 4 = 4. Students articulated the understanding that the order of the addends did not matter when adding them together; the result was the same. This realization will help these students make sense of the commutative property of addition. This strategic task encouraged students to develop justifications, or informal mathematical arguments, explaining why the number sentence was always true. The teacher also noticed that the students' initial conjecture was not clearly stated. Instead of correcting it, he provided students time to explore a counterexample for the way the conjecture was originally stated. After investigating the counterexample, students edited and revised the conjecture so that it more clearly stated why the rule was always true for the addition of zero. Additional experiences in formulating conjectures will help these students understand that conjectures stated with vague language produce misunderstandings and can be disproved with counterexamples.

Making Conjectures About Important Mathematical Ideas and Relationships

"Determining how numbers, shapes, and mathematical concepts are related is central to understanding mathematics" (Findell, Cavanagh, Dacey, Greenes, Sheffield, and Small 2004, 2). It is essential that when we choose mathematics concepts or skills for our students to begin making conjectures about, we consider students' mathematical strengths, needs, and understandings. Students cannot reason about a concept or skill they are not comfortable with or have limited knowledge of. In the previous section, we examined how asking, "Is this true?" can help generate students' reasoning that leads to the making of conjectures. These questions are excellent ways to allow students to reason about number properties of operational relationships. When students make and then examine conjectures about number operations, they deepen understandings of the relationships involved.

In the primary grades, one focus of students' mathematics typically is on odd and even numbers. Thinking about odd and even numbers encompasses a whole class of numbers, and it is important for students to make generalizations that will lead to conjectures. For example, asking students to explore the addition of two odd numbers, two even numbers, or odd and even numbers will encourage students to make conjectures about the resulting sums. These explorations build understandings necessary for thinking about other classes of numbers that students will encounter in later grades, such as prime and composite numbers, as well as factors, multiples, and divisibility rules.

We must provide students with ongoing experiences in which they are exploring the part-part-whole relationship, which is foundational for many mathematical ideas that students will encounter in later years. "To conceptualize a number as being made up of two or more parts is the most important relationship that can be developed about numbers" (Van de Walle and Lovin 2006, 43). These experiences begin in prekindergarten and should be nurtured throughout students' primary school years. The realization that six can be broken into a set of four and a set of two, a set of three and another set of three, or a set of five and a set of one promotes flexibility of number. With multiple experiences, the various parts that make up a whole are internalized by students, and these understandings support them in formulating conjectures about other mathematical ideas.

Students often devise their own way to solve a problem instead of applying a standard algorithm they do not understand. If this occurs in your discussions, encourage these students to explain why their "invented procedure" works. These procedures differ from a traditional algorithm in that they are procedures the students create because they make sense to them. Some invented procedures are applicable to every situation; however, some student-created procedures may be cumbersome and inefficient. These are all ideas worth exploring and reasoning about, and students should consider whether the invented procedure or strategy explained by a peer works every time or is efficient. The student discussions and experiences about invented procedures help them make sense of the standard algorithms.

Another important mathematical relationship students should explore and reason about is that of equality. A misconception many primary students (and older students) have about the equals sign is that it means they are to complete the calculation before it, and that the number after the equals sign is the answer. Students who think this way have not developed an understanding that the equals sign is a symbol that expresses the relationship *is the same as*. It is critical that we support students in understanding that the two values on either side of the equals sign must balance; therefore, they are the same. If students have a limited understanding of the equals sign, it creates difficulties for them in formal algebra in higher grades. It is important that students understand the correct meaning of the equals sign beginning in the early grades. But if we simply tell students the meaning of the equals sign, they will not necessarily understand it. Students must have opportunities to develop this understanding by exploring the idea through investigations. Constructing balanced equations using manipulatives is helpful, as is asking students to use materials to make equal sets. Concrete representations promote children's understandings about equality. Relating this understanding to symbolic representation remains difficult for young students, so ongoing explorations are essential. Students who have an understanding of equality are better able to do the thinking and reasoning that is necessary to make conjectures about many number relationships.

What Questions Help Students to Think About Conjectures?

Specific questions can focus students in thinking and reasoning about a mathematical relationship, which then guides them in thinking more clearly about a conjecture. Make it a priority to ask probing questions that will help your students reflect on their reasoning, especially when students' thinking needs clarification. It is crucial that we become comfortable asking questions of our students. When we are consistent in the questions we ask, it serves as a model for our students to implement when they are asking questions about other students' reasoning and proposed conjectures. The following questions can guide students in thinking about generalizations and making conjectures about them:

- What can you say about this number sentence?

- What is a rule for why this is true?

- Is it always true?

- How do you know?

- Why does this work? Will it work every time?

- If we try this with more problems, will it still work?

- Does this conjecture make sense to all of you?

- How could we revise this conjecture so that it is stated more clearly?

- What would happen if you . . . ?

Here are examples of probing questions or prompts that help to further develop and clarify a conjecture:

- Why do you agree?

- Why do you disagree?

- What did you find out when you . . . ?

- Can you give us another example of why that works?

- Can someone explain to me what was just said?

- Can you restate that reasoning in a different way?

- Will someone else restate the conjecture using your own words?

- What do you mean when you say it is always true?

- Does this conjecture make sense to you?

- What do you think about this?

Record conjectures that students make on chart paper and display them in an area of the classroom that is regularly visited by students. After a conjecture has been agreed upon by students and recorded, reread it to students so they can evaluate the conjecture as stated. A goal for students is to make their conjecture statements clear and precise. Conjectures that are unclearly stated will produce counterexamples. Ask students questions or provide prompts that model ways for students to self-monitor their reasoning and formulation of conjectures. For example:

- Does the statement make sense to you?

- Explain why you think this is true.

- Do you think this conjecture is clearly stated so a student from another classroom would understand it?

- Why did you change your mind about what you were thinking?

- What could we add to this conjecture so it would be clearer?

- Is there any part of our conjecture that needs to be taken out because it is confusing? Why do you think this is confusing?

Students will be learning that a conjecture must be precise and clearly stated so that no confusion occurs about its intent. For younger primary students, it must be written in "kid-friendly" language. As we saw demonstrated in this chapter's student dialogue, if a conjecture is too general, it causes confusion, and counterexamples can disprove it. The ability to make specific, detailed conjectures happens over time with multiple experiences. We want our students to understand that it is natural to edit and revise conjectures in order to make them clearly understandable by all. Eventually students will come to the realization that symbols can represent a conjecture more precisely than written words.

CLASSROOM-TESTED TIP

Use the word *conjecture* with older primary students. Explain that a conjecture is thinking based on unproven evidence or justification. As you begin implementing the expectation that students make conjectures about mathematical ideas, relationships, and operations, encourage them to edit and revise their conjectures in order to make them more precise. This self-monitoring of thinking is an important skill for students.

Final Thoughts

When students are making conjectures, they draw on their informal knowledge about mathematical ideas and relationships and articulate their thinking so that it becomes more explicit. With multiple experiences, students also learn that precise language is necessary to clearly state a conjecture to avoid confusion. This learning takes place when students are encouraged to reflect on their conjectures to refine them.

When students are encouraged to reflect on their thinking, it provides the support needed to reason about generalizations, which also helps in deepening their understandings of mathematics. Reflective thinking also supports students in evaluating the reasonability of the conjectures they are making as they begin to develop informal mathematical arguments to test their conjectures. It is important for students to experience situations in which counterexamples show that a conjecture is incorrect, which prompts a revision of the stated conjecture.

As you plan instruction that enables your students to reason about mathematics, you want students to make conjectures about important mathematical ideas and relationships. Choose the ideas and relationships that provide your students with experiences that will help build the foundational understandings necessary for learning mathematics in later grades. Students' examination of the properties of operations, relationships, and equality helps them understand why computation procedures work the way they do. Exploring generalizations and making conjectures about operations, relationships, and equality also allows students to connect arithmetic to algebra. These connections will help them learn algebra with understanding.

The strategy of simply asking students whether an equation is true, and then why they think so, encourages students to make conjectures about properties of operations. The use of open number sentences is effective as well for eliciting conjectures. For example, an addend is missing from this equation: $8 + 5 = \square + 6$.

Students must reason about equality to generalize how to make the number sentence true. Children with an unclear understanding of equality will likely say 13 is the answer. Providing students with a variety of open number sentences promotes reasoning, understanding of equality, and making conjectures about why the number chosen makes sense in the equation.

Questioning can focus our students' developing reasoning skills so they are better able to identify generalizations and make conjectures. Although lower-level questions have a place in our instruction in some instances, it is the higher-level questions that initiate the kind of thinking our students use to make sense of what they are learning. These questions motivate students to think, reflect, analyze, or synthesize information. A question such as "Why do you think this is true?" motivates conjecture making.

The importance of a collaborative environment for developing students' reasoning skills should not be overlooked. Asking questions such as, "What does the rest of your group think about Nick's conjecture?" and "How will you convince us that your group's reasoning is valid?" encourages students to work together to make sense of mathematics. And a question like "How does this idea relate to what we learned yesterday?" helps students connect mathematics and its applications.

Young students initially state their conjectures in words, as was demonstrated in the student dialogue. Students clarify their word choices so their conjecture makes more sense and is stated more precisely. As students' mathematical reasoning becomes more sophisticated, they see the need for describing conjectures using symbols to represent their mathematical reasoning. This awareness lays the important groundwork for students' later understanding of more formal algebraic thinking.

Questions for Discussion

1. Do you think that making conjectures is an important part of reasoning for your students? Why do you think this?

2. "Is it true?" number sentences were introduced in this chapter as a way to support students in making conjectures. What are several examples of number sentences you could present to your students to begin this process? If possible, discuss this topic with your colleagues.

3. How comfortable are you with the suggested questions in this chapter? Which questions would be the easiest to implement for you and your students? How do you see your students' role in student discussions changing with regard to questioning?

4

Developing and Evaluating
Mathematical Arguments

The ways in which children ascertain that a statement or fact in mathematics is true, accurate, and free from error evolve over time.

—Alfinio Flores, "How Do Children Know That What They Learn in
Mathematics Is True?"

The Role of Mathematical Arguments in Reasoning and Proof

A student's ability to determine that a fact or statement is true evolves over time with multiple experiences. Young children begin by basing justifications on one or several examples. In many instances, they reason that something is so simply because someone told them it was true. "To help students to reason mathematically, teachers must recognize and foster children's ability to verify for themselves whether an answer is correct, whether a procedure will produce the right answers, or whether a formula makes sense" (Flores 2002, 269).

We must expect young students to explain and justify the ideas they are reasoning about as they are problem solving. By engaging our students in these experiences in the primary grades, we are giving them the support they need to develop more sophisticated mathematical arguments in the intermediate grades and beyond. It is likely that very young students may not know why a mathematical idea is true. We must still be persistent in expecting students to explain their thinking at all times. When students begin explaining and justifying their solutions, they will do so very simply. Their justifications are based on only one or two examples. They often formulate their justifications using a strategy of trial and error, which they will eventually find unwieldy as a problem-solving strategy in later grades.

As students begin explaining and justifying their thinking and reasoning, their ideas may not be clearly understood by others. When this occurs, expect students to restate a student's explanation. This strategy is effective because it gives other students an opportunity to clarify the original student's reasoning in their own words. Restating another student's reasoning also becomes a springboard that enables students to develop justifications to either support or counter a student's initial explanation.

In Chapter 1, we shared how a first-grade teacher modeled the use of a chart to help her students organize their thinking in solving the cupcakes and brownies problem. When we introduce our students to a variety of tools that will help them organize their thinking, and provide students multiple opportunities to use them, we are giving students access to a bank of tools that allow them to make sense of the mathematics they are learning. You will find many tools on the CD that can help your students organize the thinking necessary to provide justifications for conjectures.

Our constant encouragement and support helps students to strengthen their ability to explain their thinking more thoughtfully. The experiences students have in the primary grades support them as they learn to develop justifications and mathematical arguments based on more detailed examinations of conjectures in the intermediate grades. Children's reasoning experiences in the primary and intermediate grades build the foundational understandings necessary for them to make formal proofs in higher grades.

How Can You Help Your Students Create Justifications?

The daily discussions we have with our students should include opportunities for children to explain their reasoning. Allow students to verify if their answer makes sense and to decide if a strategy used in problem solving is efficient and why this strategy is efficient. These experiences help strengthen students' abilities to self-monitor their thinking, an important aspect of reasoning. When students are explaining why a strategy they used in reaching a solution makes sense, expect them to give examples to justify their thinking. Students who are expected to explain and provide justifications are beginning the foundational skills necessary for the development of mathematical arguments.

We must consistently reinforce the expectation that students listen carefully to their classmates' reasoning so that they can determine whether an explanation is valid or whether there might be flaws in the student's thinking. Make it a habit to ask students if another student's explanation made sense, or if they have questions for the student about his explanation. This enables students to reflect on others' explanations and proposed conjectures and will allow them to better identify errors in reasoning that later may become counterexamples. Remind students that when misconceptions occur in reasoning, they should be viewed as a valuable part of mathematical thinking and reasoning. When students are encouraged to examine flaws in reasoning, they begin to develop a deeper understanding of a concept or skill. This ability to reflect on and scrutinize reasoning helps students work through difficult problem-solving situations, experiences that are beneficial for the development of their reasoning skills.

Planning experiences that include those just described provides students with opportunities to develop and evaluate explanations and justifications. By expecting students to explain why they know an answer is correct, why a problem-solving strategy always works, why a conjecture is true, or whether a justification supports or disproves a conjecture, you are giving your students many ways to convince themselves and others that the thinking and reasoning shared is valid. These experiences prepare students to tackle more formal mathematical proof-making in higher grades. (See Figure 4–1.)

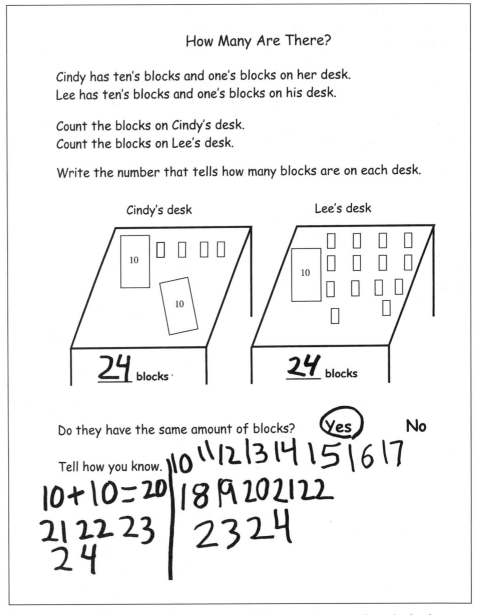

Figure 4–1 *A student uses numbers to explain her justification for why both numbers are the same.*

Questioning That Promotes the Development of Mathematical Arguments

Just as questioning is critical in helping students learn how to make conjectures, so is it important to the students' development of mathematical arguments. The questions we ask guide students in learning to think about the reasoning of others and their own reasoning as well. Students must become aware of the importance of clear explanations and justifications, which help them in developing informal mathematical arguments. Students may be confused when you first ask questions such as, "If we try this with more problems, will it still work?" They are being asked to examine what they thought was a correct response. Through encouragement, support, and our positive facilitation of student discussions, we can help them recognize the benefits of searching for justifications for why something works and makes sense.

CLASSROOM-TESTED TIP

Here are some questions that help students learn how to develop mathematical arguments:

- Why does your way of solving this problem work?

- If we try this strategy with more problems, will it still work?

- Does his explanation make sense to you?

- What part of the explanation does not make sense to you? Why?

- What would happen if you . . . ?

- How will you convince us this is true?

- Will this work if we try it with other numbers?

- What do you think will happen if you solve five more problems this way? Will the conjecture still be true?

- Do you think this strategy will work every time? Why do you think so?

- Can you think of an example that would make this not work?

Learning about what makes a valid justification occurs as students participate daily in rich discussions about the mathematics they are learning. By establishing daily discussions as a part of your classroom routine, you offer students multiple opportunities to reason, to begin noticing generalizations, and to make conjectures about a variety of mathematical ideas and relationships. Students will begin to understand that these generalizations and conjectures must first be explained so that others understand them, and then supported and justified by informal mathematical arguments. When students offer explanations and justifications, the mathematics knowledge they are learning becomes more explicit. This sense making is necessary for our students' conceptual understanding of mathematics.

Helping Students Develop and Evaluate Mathematical Arguments

In Chapter 3, we presented a student dialogue in which students formulated a conjecture about the identity property of addition. Although the purpose of the student dialogue was to engage students in the process of making conjectures, the students were beginning to develop justifications and informal mathematical arguments as they thought about the conjecture they were defending and whether or not it was always true. The ability to develop more complete mathematical arguments grows over time. The student dialogue in Chapter 1 was an example of how students were beginning to develop informal mathematical arguments. In this problem, students were investigating the possible combinations for ten cupcakes and brownies. In further exploration of the problem, students used connecting cubes to model the possible combinations. These became concrete representations of their justifications for proving they had found all the possible combinations. Although the student dialogue in Chapter 3 was not focusing on mathematical arguments, students were beginning to justify why $4 + 0 = 4$ was a true statement. These dialogues were examples of how young children begin to develop their abilities to justify ideas and conjectures in the primary grades. You may want to review the dialogues from Chapters 1 and 3 before you continue reading. In Chapter 4, we discuss what you can expect from your students as they begin learning to develop and communicate explanations and justifications that will lead to informal mathematical arguments.

CLASSROOM-TESTED TIP

Provide students with easy access to manipulatives, which are important tools for students in their early stages of developing mathematical arguments. Representing a mathematical argument with concrete materials is powerful. It helps students to visualize that a generalization can be applied to numbers or shapes without testing all cases.

In the following dialogue from a kindergarten classroom, students were justifying why the placement of the numbers 12 and 21 in a 1–50 number chart made sense. Students were shown the number chart with the two missing numbers. The missing numbers were on cards so children could place them in the number chart.

TEACHER: Think about one thing you notice on this number chart. *(Students are given about 10 seconds to do this.)* Now tell a friend what you noticed about the number chart *(about 15 seconds)*. I'd like you to share something you or a friend noticed about this chart.

STUDENT: I see a lot of numbers.

TEACHER: What numbers do you see?

STUDENT: I see a 10. That's my sister's age. I see 6, too. That's my age!

STUDENT: I can't count all of those numbers. *(Teacher asks student to count the numbers she recognizes, and she counts from 1 to 19.)*

STUDENT: The numbers go up to 50.

TEACHER: Let's count the numbers together on the number chart. *(Everyone counts from 1 to 50. This enables some students to count higher in the counting sequence than they could by themselves, and they are hearing the pattern in the count of the decade numbers.)*

STUDENT: Some numbers are missing.

TEACHER: *(Student)*, show me where the numbers are missing.

STUDENT: A number is missing from here and here.

TEACHER: I found these two numbers *(pulls two cards, 12 and 21, from her pocket)*. They fit in the spaces that don't have numbers. Talk with the person near you about where the numbers belong in the number chart.

STUDENT: We think this number fits in the first box because I counted the numbers to here. It's 12. I know because I counted.

TEACHER: Show us how you counted. *(Student counts up to 12, touching each number on the chart.)* Does anyone else have a different idea about why this number fits where *(student)* says?

STUDENT: I do! This is eleven *(points to 11 at beginning of second row of chart)*. It looks like a 1 and a 1, but it makes 11. Then it's nothing *(points to empty box)*. Here the number is 1 and 3. That's 13.

TEACHER: How does that help us know what number fits in the empty box?

STUDENT: This number has 1 and 2. I think it fits between the 1 and 1 and the 1 and 3. When we counted we said eleven, twelve, thirteen.

TEACHER: I see. You are saying that the numbers we counted right after ten had ones at the beginning of them? *(Many students agree.)*

STUDENT: We think this number *(points to 21)* is like the other number *(points to 12)*.

TEACHER: I see. Why do you think these two numbers are alike?

STUDENT: The numbers both have 2 and 1 in them.

TEACHER: What do the rest of you think about these numbers? What else do you notice?

STUDENT: Well, one number has a two in the front.

TEACHER: Show me that number.

STUDENT: You see, the 2 is here first *(points to 21)*.

TEACHER: Tell me about the other number.

STUDENT: This number has a 1 first. I think it's less than this *(21)* number.

TEACHER: How do you know that number is less?

STUDENT: I know it comes first.

TEACHER: Explain what you mean. How can we check to make sure this number comes first?

STUDENT: We can count.

TEACHER: How does counting help?

STUDENT: When you count, you'll see which number comes first. I say this number first *(pointing to 12)*. I started at one and counted it before the other one.

TEACHER: What about the other number?

STUDENT: It comes later when you count.

TEACHER: Show us what you mean when you say you counted to check.

STUDENT: 1, 2, 3, 4, 5, 6, 7, 8, 9, 10, 11, 12!

TEACHER: *(To all students)* Do you think *(student's)* explanation makes sense? *(Most agree.)* Let's put the numbers on the chart then. How can we check to see if this is the right place for the numbers? *(Students look around the room and one student points at a 100-chart.)*

STUDENT: I see the other numbers with a one first here in this row, and 12 has a one first, too. It goes in that place *(pointing after 11)*.

TEACHER: Let's say the numbers in this row. *(Students count in unison from 11 to 20.)*

STUDENT: The other number has a two first, so it goes in the row with the twos at the beginning. It goes first in the twos' row. *(See Figure 4–2.)*

TEACHER: OK, let's count from the beginning of the number chart and check that number, too. *(Students count from 1 through 50.)* I want us to be real sure we have the numbers in the right boxes. Are there other number charts in the room that we could check to see if we are right?

STUDENT: The calendar has numbers we can look at.

Figure 4–2 *A kindergarten student places 21 on a 1–50 chart after the class offers justifications for the placement of 12 and 21 on the chart.*

These kindergarten students were engaged in thinking about the correct placement of the numbers 12 and 21 in a 1–50 number chart. In a traditional classroom, students are typically asked to simply "fill in the boxes" with the correct numbers. However, this teacher's expectations that her students explain and justify why numbers were placed as they were enabled her students to think about the placement of the numbers in a more complex way. It was necessary for students to reflect on their choices in order to justify the placements. As students shared explanations and justifications, the teacher was obtaining additional information about how some students were reasoning about the task. This student dialogue demonstrated how teachers of very young children can begin to provide the mathematical situations that will support explanations and justifications. It would have been easy for the teacher to have provided a "fill-in-the-box" situation, but doing so would have hindered these students from reasoning about the task. Instead students were allowed to grapple with the problem and develop their own reasoning for how to make sense of the placement of the new numbers, which allowed them to begin to construct understandings of place value. Students were making sense of the mathematics they were learning.

CLASSROOM-TESTED TIP

A simple activity that supports students' reasoning skills is one in which students respond by answering *true* or *false* to statements similar to these*:

- *If* it is a square, *then* it must be a quadrilateral.

- *If* it is a quadrilateral, *then* it must be a trapezoid (this could be false because this statement could also be describing another type of quadrilateral).

- *If* it is a quadrilateral, *then* it must have four sides.

- *If* it is a sphere, *then* it must roll.

- *If* it is a cone, *then* it must stack.

The prior experiences that enable students to answer these types of questions more easily are sorting experiences involving two- and three-dimensional figures. In sorting experiences, students describe attributes and create sorting groups based on these attributes. Sorting into groups helps them to notice generalizations among the shapes.

Once students have decided whether a statement is true or false, they should support their reasoning with justification. Statements can be generated from a variety of mathematical ideas or relationships.

---

*This classroom-tested tip was adapted from an activity in *Teaching Student-Centered Mathematics, Grades 3–5*, by Van de Walle and Lovin (2006).

Following is a dialogue of grade 2 students reasoning about the commutative property of addition and equality. The teacher recorded a number sentence on the board and asked students, "Is this true?" In Chapter 3, this question was also the focus in a different student dialogue that provided students with the opportunity to reason about the identity property of addition. The kinds of questions that focus students toward the development of mathematical arguments are modeled for you in the dialogue that follows.

TEACHER: $2 + 3 + 4 = 3 + 4 + 2$. Is this true? What does everyone think? *(Students are given about 30 seconds.)*

STUDENT: I think it's true because it's kinda like a fact family.

TEACHER: Explain how it's like a fact family.

STUDENT: Well, three and four are seven and add 2 more, and it will be nine. Then you could add two and three, which is five and four more is nine!

TEACHER: So you're saying the three numbers add up to nine no matter which way you add them. Does anyone have anything to add to what *(student)* just said or have a question for her?

STUDENT: I agree with *(student)*. Did you do the adding in the first part only?

STUDENT: I was looking at the first part, but the other part has the same three numbers so they'll add to nine, too.

STUDENT: It's really true because if you do three plus four, it equals seven and plus two equals nine. Even if we switch all the numbers around to make four plus three plus two, it's still nine.

TEACHER: Why is this true then?

STUDENT: It's true because you just switched the same numbers around. It's not taking out numbers and putting different numbers in.

STUDENT: I thought about the equals sign. In a number sentence, what's on the left side has to be the same as what's on the right side. I checked both sides, and they're right. They both add up to nine on either side of the equals sign. And they're the same numbers in different places so you can't go wrong!

TEACHER: I think I heard you say that the equals sign is like saying *is the same as* when it's in a number sentence. *(Student agrees.)* Then we can say two plus three plus four is the same as three plus four plus two? *(Students agree.)*

TEACHER: All right, how about this number sentence: $2 + 3 + 4 = 4 + 2 + 3$? Is this true?

STUDENT: It's still true because all you did was switch the numbers around again and nothing changed except where the numbers are in the part on the right of the equals sign.

TEACHER: Hmmmm, you've almost got me convinced. I'd like you to work with a partner and write more examples to prove that you can switch numbers around and still get the same answer.

Students were given about ten minutes to work in pairs (see Figure 4–3). The teacher observed student groups as they worked to create additional examples of why this number sentence was always true. He also took advantage of this time to ask questions about how they were thinking and reasoning about the task.

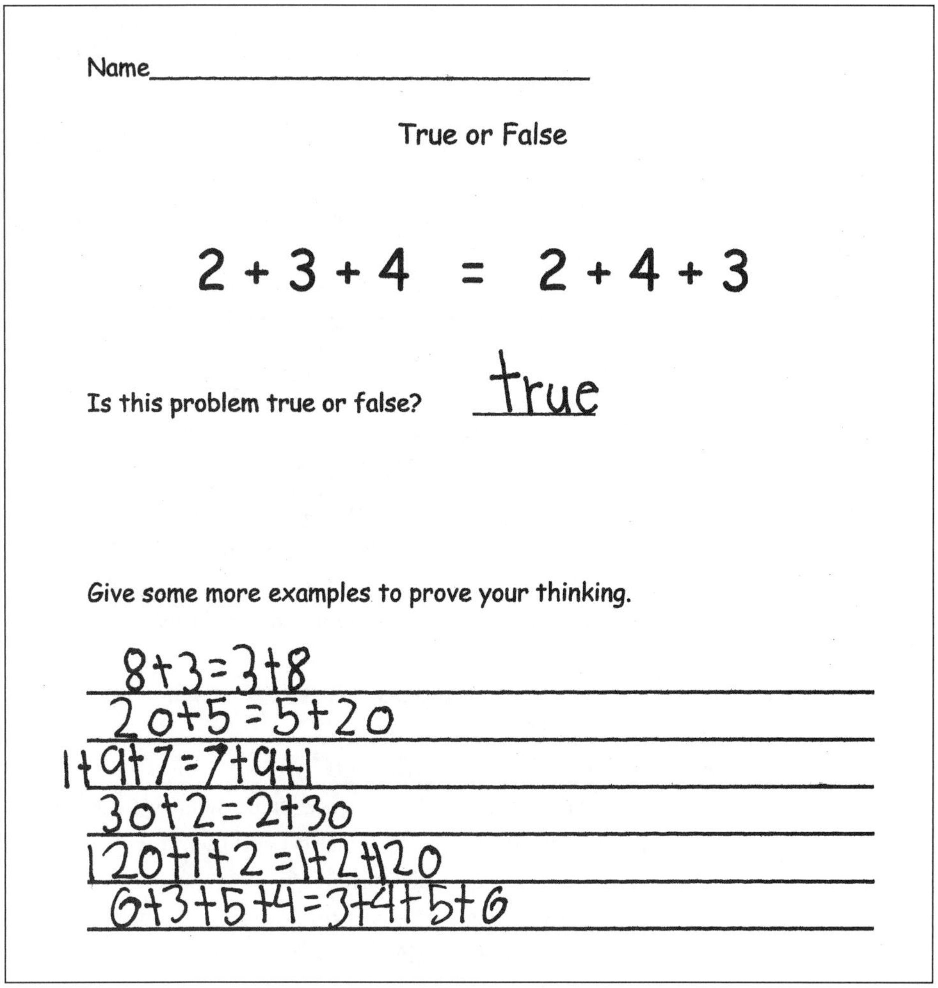

Name_____

True or False

2 + 3 + 4 = 2 + 4 + 3

Is this problem true or false? true

Give some more examples to prove your thinking.

8+3=3+8
20+5=5+20
1+9+7=7+9+1
30+2=2+30
120+1+2=1+2+120
6+3+5+4=3+4+5+6

Figure 4–3 *Additional examples generated by a student to justify the conjecture being justified by grade 2 students for why 2 + 3 + 4 = 3 + 4 + 2 is true.*

TEACHER: What do you think? Does it always work when you switch numbers around?

STUDENT: One of our examples was 5 + 3 = 8 and 3 + 5 = 8. *(More student examples are presented.)*

TEACHER: If we get rid of the " = 8" in both number sentences and write the number sentence like this, is it still true? 5 + 3 = 3 + 5. *(Students all agree.)*

STUDENT: We did 100 + 50 + 90 = 50 + 90 + 100. We're not sure what the answer is, but we know it has to be true.

STUDENT: But if you can't add them, how do you know it's true?

STUDENT: Because it's still the same three numbers on both sides. It can't add up to different answers if the same numbers are on both sides. That doesn't make sense!

STUDENT: I get it! It could be the same really high numbers in different places and still be true. You still have the same numbers to add.

STUDENT: Can we do this with subtraction?

TEACHER: OK, what does everyone think about *(student's)* question? Can we get the same results with subtraction? *(Students are not sure.)* I'd like you to talk with the person next to you about this.

STUDENT: *(after about a minute)* We don't think you can turn numbers around if you're subtracting.

TEACHER: Tell me more about what you're thinking. Why is it different with subtraction?

STUDENT: OK, it's like this: 10 – 4 = 6. Right? But if you turn the numbers around, it's 4 – 10 = 6. I started with four. I can't take ten away from four because I don't have enough.

TEACHER: Any other thoughts?

STUDENTS: It's like *(student)* said. You run out of things to take away.

TEACHER: It sounds like we are in agreement that you can't turn the same numbers around in a subtraction number sentence and still get the same answer. Is that right? *(Students agree.)* We've done a lot of thinking about why this number sentence is true when adding, and you've given examples that support your thinking. What would be our conjecture for why this is always true? *(points to the original number sentence)*

STUDENT: If you have the same numbers in different ways, it equals the same answer.

TEACHER: Is this true whether I add or subtract?

STUDENT: Wait, it doesn't work with subtraction.

TEACHER: How can we revise our conjecture so it says exactly what we mean?

STUDENT: If you switch the same numbers around, and you add them together, you'll still get the same answer. The order doesn't matter.

STUDENT: Yeah, you can put the same exact numbers on both sides of the equals sign in any order you want. It's still going to equal the same answer when you add.

Students discussed the wording of the proposed conjecture for several more minutes in their efforts to make the initial conjecture more precise. See Figure 4–4 for their final conjecture recorded by a student. It is important to note that the students' final conjecture (Figure 4–4) was still somewhat misleading since one side of the equation is not being added to the other side of the equation. During the student discussion, the teacher clearly observed that students understood why the equation was true; however, they were still having difficulty in formulating their conjecture. The teacher displayed the conjecture with plans to return to it the following day. His plans were for students to reevaluate the conjecture and decide how it could be restated more clearly to reflect their understanding of the commutative property of addition.

The teacher's intent in presenting this problem to his students was to provide a situation in which they would be encouraged to make a conjecture that required them to develop justifications to either support or disprove the conjecture. Students were experimenting with the results of moving numbers around in an equation. Number sense was also being strengthened as students discussed the meaning of the equals sign in a number sentence. One student offered a counterexample for how the explanation would not work in a subtraction situation. Although students did not understand the subtraction of numbers in a negative situation, they were considering the aspects of this process. Finally, the students who presented the example of addends

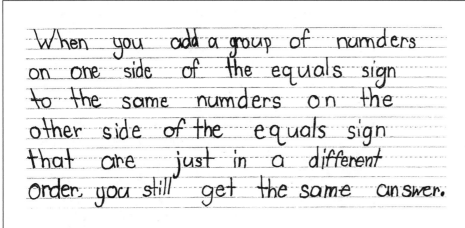

When you add a group of numbers on one side of the equals sign to the same numbers on the other side of the equals sign that are just in a different order, you still get the same answer.

Figure 4-4 *A student's recording of the class-generated conjecture about the commutative property of addition. Although it was clear to the teacher from the student dialogue that students understood the commutative property, their conjecture was misleading. Students were provided with an opportunity to revise it the following day.*

that were beyond their adding capabilities were making an important generalization that went beyond examples. They knew they didn't have to add to know the number sentence was balanced. This task enabled students not only to formulate a conjecture about the commutative property of addition, but it also enabled them to see that a counterexample could negate a proposed conjecture. This activity demonstrated the necessity for formulating conjectures that are clear and precise.

Final Thoughts

"In sum, when students make mathematical arguments, they do not simply share their answers; instead, they explain and justify the ideas that they had as they thought about and solved the problem. Explaining and justifying are important aspects of reasoning about mathematical ideas, that is, making arguments for solutions to problems" (Whitenack and Yackel 2002, 525). The ability to make mathematical arguments evolves over time. Our role is critical in the support we provide students to do this. It is essential that we provide the guidance that encourages students to listen to one another, to restate others' explanations, and to be both comfortable and respectful in questioning others' explanations and justifications.

The formal proofs that mathematicians formulate have rigorous standards. In this chapter, we have discussed the foundational understandings necessary for students so they are more ready to make more sophisticated proofs in higher mathematics. In the primary grades, students' proof making is in the form of explanations and simple justifications. Before grade 3, they are realizing that one counterexample can disprove a conjecture. A conjecture may have many examples for why it is true, but if students do not examine a conjecture for the purpose of identifying a counterexample, they may develop flawed reasoning about the conjecture. In this chapter's student dialogue, a counterexample occurred when a conjecture was not precisely stated. This result prompted students to revise their conjecture so that there would be no possibility for a counterexample. The original conjecture for why numbers could be "switched around" and still get the same answer was the following: "If you have the same numbers in different ways, it equals the same answer." Because the conjecture was not clearly stated, students were able to use a counterexample of subtraction for why this was not always true. Therefore, students edited and revised their conjecture to state: "When you add a group of numbers on one side of the equals sign to the same numbers on the other side of the equals sign that are just in a different order, you still get the same answer." We noted earlier that this conjecture will still need additional revisions to clearly convey the students' understanding of the commutative property of addition. Just as this teacher discovered, it is likely that your students' initial efforts in formulating conjectures may require multiple revisions as they attempt to precisely state what they understand to be true.

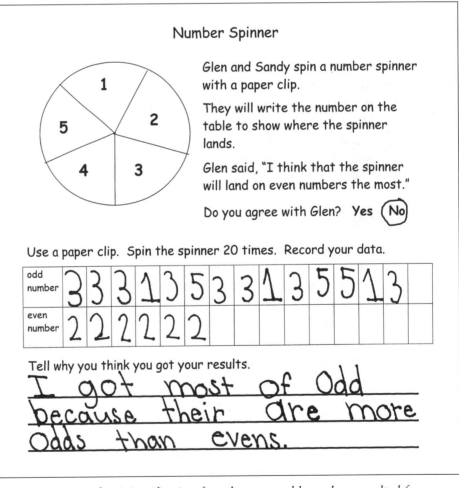

Figure 4–5 *A student's justification for why more odd numbers resulted from a CD spinner activity.*

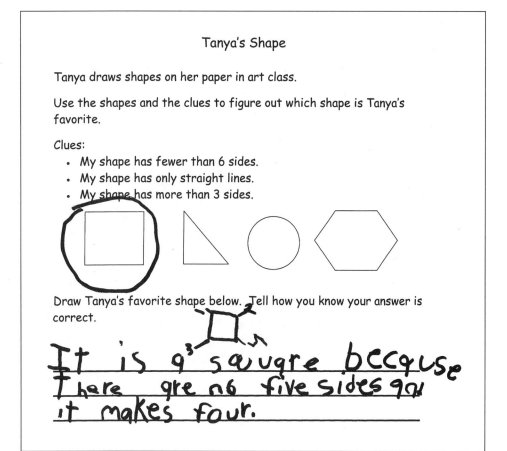

Figure 4–6 *A student solved a CD logic problem and provided justification for why his answer was correct.*

If students experience difficulties in making conjectures and developing mathematical arguments that support them, it may be because of their limited experiences in sharing explanations of reasoning. The classroom environment is a critical factor in providing a learning climate that encourages students to explain their reasoning with confidence. When students are unaccustomed to discussing and reasoning about mathematics, doing so is a challenge. Therefore, the establishment of a classroom climate that respects and nurtures our students' reasoning abilities and conveys the message that mathematics should make sense must become a high-priority goal for us.

"Justification is central to mathematics, and even young children cannot learn mathematics with understanding without engaging in justification" (Carpenter, Franke, and Levi 2003, 85). To understand mathematical ideas and relationships, students must use explanations, justifications, and informal arguments to convince themselves and others that their reasoning is valid. The role that has traditionally described teachers is that of the giver of all mathematical procedures and rules, and the role assigned to students is to be the recipients of this information. These traditional roles inhibit students' development of reasoning abilities. In a standards-based instructional program, students are encouraged to explore mathematical ideas. (See Figures 4–5 and 4–6.) Students who are engaged in meaningful mathematical learning routinely reason and make sense of what they are learning, notice generalizations, develop conjectures about mathematical ideas and relationships, and test their conjectures with justifications and informal mathematical arguments. These kinds of reasoning skills empower our students to become mathematical thinkers who understand that mathematics is about sense making.

Questions for Discussion

1. Reflect on or discuss with your colleagues: What is the importance of allowing students the opportunity to explain their thinking and to present justifications that will lead to more complex mathematical arguments in higher grades?

2. How does the process of making mathematical arguments help students to deepen their reasoning abilities?

3. What are some of the challenges that may occur as you begin to adjust your mathematics instruction to include (a) experiences for students that will support them in stating conjectures and (b) time to make informal mathematical arguments that will either support or disprove these conjectures?

4. Discuss with your colleagues: What actions can you take to make the challenges identified in question 3 more manageable?

CHAPTER 5

How the Process Standards Support Reasoning and Proof

Learning with understanding can be further enhanced by classroom inter-actions, as students propose mathematical ideas and conjectures, learn to evaluate their own thinking and that of others, and develop mathematical reasoning skills.

—National Council of Teachers of Mathematics,
Principles and Standards for School Mathematics

The process standards described by the National Council of Teachers of Mathematics are the ways students learn and apply their mathematical content knowledge. We have discussed the process standard of reasoning and proof in great detail. Now we will explore how the remaining process standards—problem solving, communication, representation, and connections—relate to and support reasoning and proof. The process standards are highly interconnected and support one another. The five process standards are integrated throughout our daily lessons as we provide experiences for our students to develop understandings of the five content standards—number and operations, algebra, geometry, measurement, and data analysis and probability.

Problem Solving

Problem solving and reasoning are highly dependent on one another. "Students who can both develop and carry out a plan to solve a mathematical problem are exhibiting knowledge that is much deeper *and* more useful than simply carrying out a computation" (NCTM 2000, 182). The way students think and reason about a problem-solving situation supports this deeper understanding and thus helps support their reasoning. NCTM has recommended that instructional programs from prekindergarten through grade 12 include experiences that enable students to learn new mathematics in a problem-solving manner. Problem solving should occur daily, not only in our mathematics instruction but throughout students' school day. When we take advantage of those mathematical moments that occur outside of our math class time, we are providing our students with real-life applications of the mathematics they are learning.

NCTM also has recommended that students have multiple opportunities to apply many ways to solve problems, so they may become flexible in how they think about mathematics. In today's classrooms, students should be able to self-monitor their problem-solving strategies for effectiveness. It is important that they reflect on why a strategy works for a particular problem, which strategy is more efficient than others for a wide range of problems, and how to refine a strategy that is not efficient. Students will be taking ownership of the mathematics they are learning.

Problem solving is the vehicle for learning mathematical knowledge. If students cannot make important decisions about solving problems, all the procedures and facts they have learned are of little use. The problems we present to our students must be engaging and challenging and provide opportunities for students to reason about mathematical ideas and relationships. We want students to understand that problem solving may take time, which encourages them to be persistent problem solvers. The cupcakes and brownies problem in Chapter 1 is an example of this type of problem solving. In this problem, students were mathematically involved in an interesting task in which they were identifying all the possible combinations for ten desserts that their teacher could send to her brother. The problem was presented in the familiar context of a birthday celebration. Students were challenged to explain the reasoning they used to determine when they had identified all combinations. Engaging problems that allow students to grapple with the solutions both support and develop their reasoning abilities. Tackling challenging problems may prove difficult for some students at first; therefore, we must know when it is time to assist our students as they struggle with a problem. Providing assistance too soon will inhibit our students from reasoning and making valuable mathematics revelations about their problem solving. By skillfully posing questions in our conversations, we can help them consider and reflect on ideas as they are working through the problem-solving situation.

Our students' disposition toward problem solving is important to consider as it affects their ability to persevere in a problem-solving situation. Students with a positive disposition are flexible in their thinking, take risks that are reasonable, are able to self-monitor their thinking, and test ideas about their thinking and reasoning. We begin to develop these characteristics of positive disposition in young children when we present them with multiple problem-solving opportunities that are fun, engaging, and challenging. Offering students rich and thought-provoking problems helps them become confident problem solvers who also use reasoning to solve and make sense of all kinds of mathematical situations. It is crucial that we allow young children to rethink a problem and that we are careful not to give a quick answer that ends the process of thinking and problem solving.

The following student dialogue is an example of how the use of tools can help students organize their thinking in order to solve complex problems. The tool used in this instance was a matrix. The students in this second-grade classroom were solving a logical-thinking problem that focused on number concepts. The teacher's initial intent was to provide students with an opportunity to solve a challenging problem that would help them develop their reasoning skills. She was introducing and modeling the use of a matrix as a problem-solving tool. The teacher posted the problem and clues on the blackboard, which would allow students to revisit the problem as they considered all the clues. The following statements were read to students:

> Terry, Emma, Billy, Jack, and Alan have 15 books altogether.
> They each have a different number of books.
> Jack has only one book.
> Emma has the most books.
> Emma and Billy together have a total of seven books.
> Terry has one book less than Alan.

After allowing time for students to talk about the clues with a partner, the teacher initiated the following discussion:

TEACHER: You've had time to discuss the clues with a partner. What clue would help us begin to solve this problem?

STUDENT: I think the clue about Jack.

TEACHER: Explain why you chose that clue.

STUDENT: That clue says Jack has only one chapter book.

TEACHER: So that is something we know for sure. Take a look at this chart. It's called a matrix, and it can help us organize the information we are figuring out from the clues. How could we show that Jack has only one book?

STUDENT: Mark in the square next to his name.

TEACHER: *(She calls on another student.)* Do you agree with (student)?

STUDENT: That's right because on the top it says one book. So make a mark in the box under it and next to Jack's name.

TEACHER: How shall I record that we know Jack has one book?

STUDENT: Let's do a smiley face. We're happy we figured out the clue! *(Teacher records a smiley face in box.)*

TEACHER: All right, let's think about the problem again. It says they each have a different number of books, so could Emma have one book?

CLASS: No!

TEACHER: In a matrix, we can record what a person does not have. That helps us when we think about the other clues. What should I write to show that Emma does not have one book?

STUDENT: I think a big, fat X!

TEACHER: What does everyone think?

CLASS: Yes!

STUDENT: We need to make more X's.

TEACHER: What do you mean?

STUDENT: Well, Jack is the only one with one book so everyone else can have an X.

TEACHER: What clue shall we use next?

STUDENT: Use Emma's clue. She has the most chapter books.

TEACHER: So how many books does Emma have?

STUDENT: She has the most books and five is the largest number. Emma has the five books.

TEACHER: So we'll put a smiley face under five in the same row as Emma's name.

STUDENT: That means Emma can't have two, three, or four books.

STUDENT: And she can't have one book because Jack does.

TEACHER: How can we show what Emma can't have? *(Student approaches matrix and records X's in the appropriate boxes to show what Emma does not have. Then students place X's in the correct boxes to eliminate the other students under the five column.)* Then she asks students to restate what they know.

STUDENT: Jack has one book, and Emma has five books. We don't know who has two, three, or four books.

STUDENT: Let's do the next clue.

TEACHER: OK, Emma and Billy together have a total of seven books.

STUDENT: Billy has two books because five plus two equals seven.

TEACHER: What does everyone think? *(All agree.)* Wait a minute, I'm confused. Three and four equal seven, too. How do you know that Billy definitely has two books?

STUDENT: Because Emma and Billy put their books together and got seven books. Emma has five books because there's a smiley face in her box under five books. Five and two more is seven. Billy has two books.

STUDENT: I think Alan has four books.

TEACHER: How do you know?

STUDENT: The clue says Terry has one book less than Alan. The only spots left are three and four. Three is one less than four. It has to be Terry with three and Alan with four books.

Students were beginning to use deductive reasoning to eliminate each of the clues until they were able to identify all the answers to the logic problem. Mathematics vocabulary was prevalent throughout the discussion, and students were using their knowledge about number concepts to help them analyze the clues (*most, combinations of seven, less*). (See Figure 5–1.) This was the first time students had used a matrix to solve a logic problem. In this particular problem, students were able to solve the problem by thinking about the clues in sequential order. In more difficult logic problems, students can consider clues out of order when deductively reasoning about the problem's outcomes. Although the teacher's initial intent was simply to provide a problem-solving situation that required reasoning, the following was also occurring for students:

■ Students were engaged in simple deductive reasoning.

■ Students were reinforcing ideas about number, specifically their ability to think logically.

■ The teacher modeled a problem-solving tool for students that helped them organize their thinking so they could solve a difficult problem.

Figure 5–1 *Grade 2 students review the results of using a matrix to problem solve
a logical thinking problem about chapter books.*

- Students were developing their ability to communicate mathematically.

- The teacher was helping students develop important components of effective mathematical disposition: (1) Students reflected on choices they were making to determine if they made sense. (2) Students took risks when they expressed reasoning for choices. (3) Students tested and compared ideas as the problem was solved.

- The teacher obtained important information about her students' problem-solving abilities and how they were reasoning about the problem.

The activities provided for you on the CD are problems that will be both engaging and thought provoking for your students. They will help your students strengthen their number sense, problem solving, and reasoning abilities. Whether you allow your students to complete these problems as a whole group, in small groups, or independently, the discussions you facilitate with students are critical. If students will sometimes be completing the activities independently, it is important to bring students back together to discuss their problem solving and reasoning strategies. These discussions give students opportunities to share multiple strategies and talk about the reasoning they are using in solving the problems. And you will learn a lot about your students' understandings!

In the beginning, students may begin by sharing more procedural strategies as they explain the different ways they solved the problems. In addition to focusing on how a problem was solved, encourage your students to discuss why the strategy used in the problem solving makes sense. Gradually you will want to guide the discussions in such a way that you are supporting students in developing explanations and justifications that support the reasoning they are learning to develop. The discussions you have with your students will be a source for informal assessments of how students are reasoning about mathematical ideas and relationships.

Communication

The process standard of communication plays a critical role in supporting reasoning and proof. Talking and writing are the ways that students make their thinking about mathematics visible and explicit. NCTM has recommended that instructional programs from prekindergarten through grade 12 include experiences that enable students to communicate the mathematics they are learning in a variety of ways. In order for students to effectively communicate their thinking and reasoning, they must first organize this thinking. This is also true when students communicate in writing. In prekindergarten through grade 2, it is crucial for students to communicate ideas and reasoning so that others clearly understand their thinking.

Young children begin by using verbal and nonverbal strategies to communicate their mathematical thinking to us. They use their fingers, draw pictures, or show us how they are thinking with manipulatives. In their verbal descriptions, they use informal language to describe how they are making sense of the math they are learning. We can support students' developing communication skills in several ways: (1) In our daily discussions, we can connect their informal language to mathematics vocabulary that is more accurate. (2) We can listen carefully to their verbal descriptions and encourage clarity when appropriate. (3) We must model good communication skills for our students. (4) We must expect that students listen to other students' explanations. (5) Finally, we must provide students with many opportunities to practice a variety of communications skills.

We should also make it a priority to communicate with our students in multiple ways. Since students in the early years of this grade band are not reading fluently, we can help by reading directions to them or creating drawings to represent steps in thinking about a task.

Reasoning and proof are interconnected and highly dependent upon the communication standard. This relationship has been demonstrated for you in the student dialogue examples throughout this book. In these dialogues, we have observed students communicating in collaborative groups in order to problem solve together. When students are presented with opportunities to talk about mathematics, it helps them to reflect on what they are learning and to make sense of it. The dialogues throughout the book demonstrate how teachers can help students develop communication skills when they restate what students have said or when they ask other students to do the same, which validates students' thinking. Teachers also connect students' informal mathematical thinking to more formal mathematics. When we ask probing questions and describe what we observe our students doing, it supports them as they strengthen their abilities to communicate their reasoning process.

In addition, the discussions we facilitate with our students provide us with important information about what our students understand about the math we are teaching them. It is easier to recognize a student's misconception when it is revealed in a student discussion rather than left unspoken in a classroom where discourse is not an expectation. The knowledge you acquire about how your students are reasoning and making sense of mathematics provides you with invaluable information that allows you to plan instruction that meets the needs of all your students.

CLASSROOM-TESTED TIP

There are several ways to organize your students to enhance student discourse. These formats should vary according to the needs of your students and your instructional goals for the lesson.

■ A whole-group discussion is demonstrated in many of the student dialogues presented in this book. During these discussions, the teacher acted as a facilitator to guide students' thinking and reasoning. Instead of the focus being only on the answer, the focus was on how students were thinking and reasoning about the process used to reach the solution. These whole-group discussions provide students with essential experiences that support their development of reasoning skills.

■ Small groups are utilized when students have begun in a whole-group discussion but there is a need to move into smaller groups to further investigate the mathematics. In several of the student dialogues demonstrated, students began as a whole group and then formed smaller groups to further discuss the task. In small-group discussions, the teacher circulates among the groups as students engage in mathematical tasks. Instead of controlling these discussions, our role should be that of an observer. And as an observer, we can assist students' learning by redirecting their thinking if necessary. This is a time to informally converse with students about their problem solving. The observations and conversations provide us with a way to informally assess how our students are reasoning.

■ The last format for discourse is partner talk. In this format, the teacher asks a question and provides partners a short amount of time to discuss it together. This format is usually implemented within a whole-group discussion. If you find that wait time is not producing student talk in a whole-group discussion, a change to partner talk might help. Partner talk is especially beneficial for students who are not comfortable talking in front of a larger group. It gives students time to talk in a less threatening environment. If a student is confused, he'll be more likely to talk about this confusion with a peer. Students who are learning to speak English find that partner talk helps them to adjust to their new situation. The short time that you provide for students to talk with a partner prepares all your students to take a more active role in a whole-group discussion.

In the sample student dialogues provided in previous chapters, we have demonstrated students reasoning about a variety of mathematics topics. In these experiences, students were given wait time. This strategy allowed them an opportunity to reflect on their thinking and thus encouraged reasoning. When students worked in small groups or talked with a partner, these experiences also helped them to organize and hear different interpretations of reasoning within their groupings. Students were learning to clarify their conjectures, explanations, and justifications when they were asked to restate their own thinking or the thinking of others. In the student dialogues, the use of mathematical language was modeled by the teachers and the students. Specific questions that encouraged student reasoning were modeled by the teachers.

It is important to point out that the student discourse occurring in these classrooms was a result of established routines. The ability to discuss mathematics meaningfully develops over time. In Chapter 1, we shared important factors that you should consider when establishing student discourse as a routine in your classroom. One of the most important factors that directly affects the success of student discourse is the climate or environment of a classroom. We establish the climate at the beginning of each school year, and our goal should be to create a community that allows students to feel safe and comfortable. Our students will be more likely to take risks and share reasoning in this type of a learning community than in one that feels competitive or unsafe. Students in a supportive environment will not feel threatened if they learn that their reasoning contains flaws, and the opportunities to further examine and analyze these misconceptions will enhance your students' developing mathematical learning.

It is important that students understand how your classroom environment and routines are organized. In order for student discourse to become a productive routine, we must clearly explain our expectations about the students' role in these discussions. You may find that for some students, participating in student discussions will be a new and perhaps an intimidating experience. When students know and understand what is expected of them, it provides them with a rationale for why and how they are to communicate reasoning in your classroom discussions.

CLASSROOM-TESTED TIP

The following expectations are important for your students to understand about their participation in student discussions:

- Students will communicate their thinking to you and to other students.

- Students will question you and other students to help them clarify their own thinking.

- Students must explain and justify their thinking and reasoning.

- Students will view flawed reasoning or misconceptions as learning opportunities.

Many teachers find it difficult to transition from a classroom oriented mainly toward teacher talk to one oriented toward student talk. As you begin to encourage and support more student talk, you may hear students sharing thinking and reasoning that is flawed or consists of misconceptions. Teachers often express that they find it difficult to know how to respond to a student's flawed reasoning. Understanding the mathematics we are teaching students will help. To help our students sort through their misconceptions, it is necessary that we are aware of more than the basic skills, rules, and procedures of mathematics. It is critical that we understand how students develop conceptual understanding of the mathematical concepts and skills we are teaching. This deeper understanding of the mathematics we are teaching will support us in facilitating student discussions in which flawed reasoning may occur.

Planning with colleagues in grade-level team meetings provides you with opportunities to discuss how students conceptually develop understandings about mathematics. These understandings have more depth than that of a memorized rule or procedure. Identify the prerequisites of the concepts and skills that students will be learning in a particular topic. This information will help you to determine whether students have sufficient understandings about the mathematics to be learned. As you informally observe students, you can determine whether a student has gaps in her learning about a concept or skill. Note these informal observations to help in planning with your team.

Discuss how the grade level's objectives develop understandings for concepts and skills that will be learned in later grades. These planning times with your grade-level colleagues will help guide your facilitation of discussions with students. When students demonstrate that they are missing key understandings necessary for the grade level's objectives, or when students contribute information that is beyond what is being taught, you will be prepared to address these issues.

When beginning any new topic in mathematics, discuss with your grade-level team any misconceptions you think your students may have about the mathematical concepts. Identifying potential misunderstandings helps you to plan your lessons. You will be better able to redirect students' thinking and reasoning if you have an understanding of what these misconceptions could be.

Even though we have emphasized how important it is to have less teacher talk, our role remains essential in the student discussions we facilitate. We must ensure that student discussions flow in a focused manner and that we ask probing questions to promote reasoning, which will enable us to delve deeper into how our students are thinking. We must convey a message to our students that mathematics is about sense making, and students should know that their thinking and reasoning about mathematics are valued.

In addition to discourse, writing is an effective communication strategy for supporting reasoning and proof. When students write about their thinking and reasoning, they must reflect, clarify, and then organize their thinking in order to write about it. Their writing is a record of their thinking, and it becomes a tool that helps them to analyze and reflect on the mathematics they are writing about. Writing is a way for student to internalize ideas about mathematics. Equally important is that our students' writing provides us with another glimpse of how they are reasoning and reveals the understandings or misconceptions they may hold about mathematical ideas and relationships.

Before students can be expected to write about mathematics, they must first talk about mathematics. Students benefit from multiple experiences in which they are talking about mathematical ideas and strategies. These experiences provide the foundation needed to write meaningfully about mathematics.

Math journals are often used to encourage students to write about the ideas they are learning in mathematics. They are beneficial for students because they provide a chronological journal of their mathematical learning during the school year. In order for students to write about mathematics, they must first reflect on the mathematics from the activity, which then helps them to organize their thinking. Students will be thinking about what was done with the mathematics during the lesson and what was required to complete the problem solving in the activity. Math journal writing is effective when it occurs immediately after a student discussion because students have had an opportunity to talk about the mathematics they will be writing about in their journal. It is difficult for students to write about something they have not discussed.

Math journals can also be used in the beginning of a lesson. Ask students to write what they already know about the concept that is the focus of that day's lesson, or what they think they will learn about the concept and why they think this. Another use of journals is to help you determine what the students understand about a specific concept or skill. Ask them to select what was the most difficult part of the math lesson and to explain how they reasoned about it.

The feedback we provide to students in their math journals should be specific and helpful to their continued mathematics learning. Feedback that is vague tells students little about their thinking and reasoning. Simply writing "Good Job!" on a student's journal entry does not tell what about the reasoning was good. It is not necessary to write feedback in students' math journals every day, but when you do provide feedback to your students, include specific details that help them know how they are progressing in their reasoning and thinking about mathematics. Here are a few examples of specific feedback:

■ Please explain how you estimated to solve this problem.

■ You gave many examples for why this problem makes sense.

■ Your pictures show you understand odd and even numbers.

■ What do you think will happen if you try it with two-digit numbers?

■ Placing the coins in a list helped you think about this problem.

A writing format that students enjoy is writing a letter to an absent student about the mathematics learned from that day's lesson. (See Figure 5–2.) Students write about the reasoning discussed during the lesson's problem-solving activity or explain what

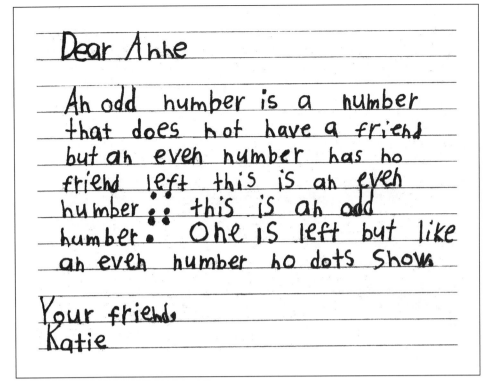

Dear Anne

An odd number is a number
that does not have a friend
but an even number has no
friend left this is an even
number :: this is an odd
number : One is left but like
an even number no dots show

Your friend,
Katie

Figure 5–2 *A second-grade student writes to an absent student to explain what was learned in that day's math lesson about odd and even numbers. The last sentence explains that an odd number would be even if an extra dot was drawn.*

CLASSROOM-TESTED TIP

Suggestions for math journal prompts:

■ What was easy in the math we did today? Why?

■ What was hard in the math we did today? Why?

■ How would you tell a friend to solve this problem?

■ Explain why your way of solving the problem makes sense.

■ Finish this sentence: I wish I knew more about . . .

■ Explain why the conjecture we discussed today is always true.

■ Explain why you think your reasoning is correct.

they understand about the mathematics in the activity. A teacher reading this letter would learn important information about the student's thinking. Students' letters can also be a type of informal assessment for the teacher. Letters allow you to monitor students' understandings about the concepts and skills they are learning, which guide you in planning instruction. Of course, letters should also be shared with the absent student! This writing activity then becomes purposeful, and it helps students understand the importance of describing mathematical thinking and reasoning clearly so that others will understand it.

CLASSROOM-TESTED TIP

Here are several strategies for supporting students in writing about how they are thinking and reasoning:

- Talking helps. If a large-group discussion is not possible first, ask students to discuss a task with a partner before writing, for example, in a journal.

- Before students submit a writing assignment, expect students to review and revise their explanation of reasoning.

- Invite students to share their written explanations of reasoning. This helps them to identify any ideas that are not clearly explained. Provide a "mathematician's chair" for students to sit in when they are sharing their reasoning.

Opportunities for students to write about mathematical understandings are provided in the various CD activities. In many of these activities, students write to explain their reasoning in solving a problem. These writing experiences benefit students because they are writing to convince the reader that their reasoning in the problem solving is correct and to explain why it is correct. These writing responses will provide you with informal assessment information about how your students are solving and reasoning about a variety of tasks. Reading their responses will provide you with opportunities to later ask students questions about how they thought about problems in order to solve them. When students' writing responses reveal misconceptions or flaws in their reasoning, you can use this information to help these students.

CLASSROOM-TESTED TIP

Teachers of prekindergarten and kindergarten children can record students' learning from a mathematical experience by recording the group's contributions on chart paper. Many teachers begin by incorporating words students are familiar with and then drawing pictures for words that are beyond their reading capabilities. As students are dictating, they will see their verbalizations becoming a written form of communication. This type of early writing could also become a class letter to an absent student or to another person at the school, such as the principal.

We have briefly discussed the importance of providing feedback on students' writing responses. It is vital to provide specific feedback that is precise and helps students to further reflect on the mathematics they are learning. When a student receives a response of "Great" or "Super," it does not specifically provide them with informational feedback about their thinking and reasoning, and it discourages them from further reflecting on their reasoning. Provide feedback that tells students exactly how their reasoning is effective. When a student's writing response includes flawed reasoning, our response must redirect their thinking so that they will reflect on and analyze the flaws. This revision process will enable them to develop a clearer understanding of their original reasoning. Even though we may not have time to provide feedback on every student's writing assignment, reading all of our students' writing assignments is essential. These writing assignments provide informative evidence of what our students understand about a particular mathematics idea at that point in time. They are visible evidence of mathematical learning that we can also share with parents.

Representation

In the early childhood years, we must offer our students opportunities to represent their mathematical ideas in a variety of ways; therefore, the classroom environment should encourage the use of multiple representations. Young students' representations include concrete objects, pictorial drawings, physical gestures, graphical representations such as pictographs or bar graphs, and symbols (Greenes 1999).

The process standard of representation supports students' reasoning in several ways. The models or representations that students develop are a connection between a mathematics concept and the symbols used to explain that concept. The representations help them create a mental picture of a mathematical idea, and students will be applying their concrete learning to the more abstract aspects of mathematics. Allowing students to choose how to represent their thinking and reasoning about a mathematical idea helps them to make sense of the mathematics they are learning. This eventually enables students to choose among representations to demonstrate reasoning about a particular mathematics idea. Giving students the freedom to decide which representation will appropriately convey their understanding encourages them to think flexibly.

Students' representations demonstrate their understandings about mathematical relationships and reveal their reasoning to us. Students utilize representations as tools to problem solve, communicate thinking, and express mathematical ideas, and these representations can be used to support or disprove conjectures. Representing thinking enables students to organize and make sense of their thinking and reasoning. (See Figure 5–3.) NCTM has recommended that instructional programs in prekindergarten through grade 12 include experiences that enable students to make a variety of representations to help them think and reason about mathematics.

"Good representations fulfill a dual role: they are tools for thinking and instruments for communicating" (NCTM 2000, 206). When students represent their reasoning, it affords them opportunities to visualize their thinking. The ability to visualize thinking is important when student's initial reasoning is incorrect. This flawed

Barbara's 8 Color Tiles

Barbara has 8 color tiles.
Read the clues to figure out how many blue, red and yellow tiles Barbara has.

- $\frac{1}{2}$ of her tiles are red.
- One of her tiles is blue.
- The rest of her tiles are yellow.

Use tiles help you figure out how many tiles of each color Barbara has.

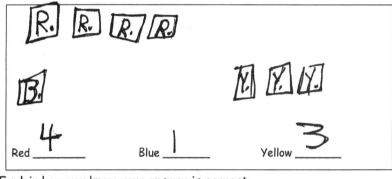

Red ___4___   Blue ___1___   Yellow ___3___

Explain how you know your answer is correct.

I know my answer is correct because the reds have to be four because four is half of eight. I know I need one blue tile. So 4+1=5 so I need 3 yellows.

Figure 5–3 *This student drew a representation and wrote to explain his reasoning for the correct answer to this CD task.*

reasoning may not be apparent to the student if she has not had the opportunity to view the reasoning in a representation. Students' representations help them remember and reflect on what they did in the mathematical task, extend their thinking, and justify their reasoning to others.

Technology is another type of representation young students are capable of using effectively. Students should understand that representations involve more than just *showing* how a problem is solved. It is important for our students to understand that representations are tools that help them develop understandings about mathematical ideas and that these representations communicate information about their thinking and reasoning in an organized manner. When analyzing students' representations, we cannot assume we know what a student understands about a concept or skill that is being represented. It is therefore important that we expect a student to explain any representation to us, which presents us with more accurate information on what the student understood.

As mentioned earlier, we want students to understand that some representations are more useful than others. We can support our students in determining the most appropriate way to represent their reasoning by presenting different representations and discussing with them which representations are more effective in describing and justifying their reasoning. When students are first learning to represent a conjecture they do so in words. Eventually they will find that a conjecture is more precisely stated in a symbolic representation. Students should become comfortable in using a variety of representations so they are able to choose those that are more useful for reasoning about different mathematical situations.

Connections

As students develop reasoning about mathematical ideas and relationships, they are forming connections from previously learned knowledge in a variety of areas. "These connections help students see mathematics as a unified body of knowledge rather than as a set of complex and disjoint concepts, procedures, and processes" (NCTM 2000, 200). In the connection process standard, NCTM has recommended that instructional programs in prekindergarten through grade 12 include experiences that enable students to see how a mathematics concept relates to other mathematical ideas, how these ideas overlap one another and build on one another, how mathematics is connected to other disciplines such as social studies or science, and how mathematics applies to their lives outside of school.

Connections are naturally present in an early childhood classroom. Some connections are discovered by children, but we also need to make connections apparent to students as they are learning. Many connections occur during daily classroom routines such as calendar or center time. It is critical that we provide experiences for our students that will enable them to appreciate the rich connectedness of mathematics. Students in prekindergarten through grade 2 should be reasoning about mathematical ideas and relationships found in real-world situations, among mathematics, and across other disciplines. The reasoning that students connect to their everyday lives will prepare them for making decisions in future years. When students see connections across mathematical concepts, it helps them understand that mathematics consists of closely connected ideas that support one another. For example, this becomes apparent when students must apply their knowledge of number to help them measure in different ways. Mathematics is naturally integrated in science, technology, social studies, and geography.

Our role is to help our students make connections by guiding them to see these connections in a variety of contexts and models. Connections must be made in a natural way rather than in a contrived manner. Connections that are natural allow young children to develop mathematical understandings meaningfully. The connections our students are able to make with our support will help them refine their reasoning in a broader sense. A very simple way to approach this is encouraging students to look for how mathematics is used throughout the school day, at home, or in their community. When students apply reasoning to everyday contexts, it provides them with a rationale for why mathematics should make sense and why it is important.

Following is a kindergarten discussion of the monthly weather graph that was part of the students' calendar routine. The teacher routinely uses the calendar activities as a springboard for making mathematical connections in a variety of ways. Throughout the previous month, students recorded the weather for each school day as sunny, cloudy, rainy, or snowy.

TEACHER: What do you notice about our weather graph? Tell a friend what you notice about the weather from last month. *(Students are given a minute to do this.)*

STUDENT: We had a lot of sun days.

TEACHER: How do you know that?

STUDENT: I can see there are more tally marks by the sun pictures. The other pictures don't have as many marks.

STUDENT: The snow days did not have any.

TEACHER: Explain what you mean.

STUDENT: The picture of the snow did not have any marks after it.

TEACHER: Would you have needed to wear snow boots or sandals last month?

STUDENT: I think we could wear sandals. There is no snow.

STUDENT: I have boots for the rain.

STUDENT: Sometimes the sun is out, and it's cold! Maybe I would wear boots on that day.

TEACHER: What information from the weather graph made you think about rain boots?

STUDENT: The picture of the rain had some marks so it was raining on some of the days. I have pink boots for the rain.

TEACHER: Look at the graph. Which type of weather happened on the most days?

STUDENT: Sunny days had the most.

TEACHER: How can we check to see if what *(student)* says is true?

STUDENT: You can count to see if it is more than the other weather.

STUDENT: There are more marks for sun days. It is longer so it has more.

TEACHER: How can we figure out which type of weather happened the least?

STUDENT: The rain days were less.

TEACHER: Do we all agree that we had rain the least amount of days?

STUDENT: No, the rain is not less. It's the snow.

TEACHER: How do you know?

STUDENT: Look. Snow days has zero. That is less than the rain days.

TEACHER: What does zero mean?

STUDENT: It means nothing! And there's not one mark for the snow days.

TEACHER: Well, is everyone else sure about what zero means?

STUDENT: Yeah, because on the counting chart the zero is smaller than five.

TEACHER: I see that. Thank you for showing us that. Explain again how that helps us figure out that the amount of snow days was less than the days for rain.

STUDENT: There were five rain days and zero comes before five when you count, so it's less. It is even less than one!

TEACHER: Help me figure out the numbers of days for each type of weather so we can put the weather pictures in order from the most to the least. *(Students count together the days for each type of weather. They record the numbers on paper.)*

TEACHER: Which type of weather did we have the most last month?

STUDENT: Sunny had the most. It had nine days, and that's a bigger number than any of the others.

TEACHER: What do the rest of you think? Is nine a larger number than the other numbers we counted?

STUDENT: Yeah, the other numbers are counted before the nine so that makes nine bigger than them.

STUDENT: Cloudy is second.

TEACHER: How do you know that?

STUDENT: Well, it's seven. Seven is two under nine.

TEACHER: Explain what you mean.

STUDENT: Count backwards. Start at nine and go back two times . . . eight, seven!

STUDENT: Snowy has to be last because it's zero.

STUDENT: Rainy is next to last because it had five days. That's the number before six and seven, so it's smaller than seven.

The teacher began the data discussion by asking students an open-ended question, "What do you notice about our weather graph?" This allowed students to interpret the graph in their own ways. The students in this classroom naturally compared the quantities displayed on the graph. These conversations led to several concepts about number such as more and less, the meaning of zero, and the language of math. They briefly discussed and reasoned that snow boots could be worn on snowy days as well as sunny days that were perhaps cold. The teacher encouraged students to explain their reasoning in determining how they knew which type of weather occurred the most or least. Students were also asked to numerically sequence the number of days each type of weather occurred. This promoted reasoning as they explained the placement of each number in the sequence. (See Figure 5–4.) The data discussion in the teacher's calendar routine helped her make meaningful connections to her students' everyday lives and to other mathematical concepts and skills.

Sometimes in making connections for our students, it may be necessary to plan ahead to highlight mathematics where appropriate. Participating in grade-level team planning to focus on these connections will help you more easily accomplish this task. Focus on mathematics that is useful for students to apply in their everyday lives. (See Figure 5–5.) Science is a discipline in which mathematics is highly integrated with reasoning, which is a critical part of any scientific investigation. Disciplines such as social studies rely on mathematics for certain ideas. An example of an everyday connection in social studies is when students are using directional and positional words to describe locations on a map. For example, "My house is on the left side of the library." or "The library is shown above the lake on the map." This is a practical application of mathematics and may even stop the question "When will I ever use this math?"

Utilizing children's literature is an excellent strategy to help students make connections in mathematics. Math-related literature books are engaging and present students with problem-solving situations that involve real-world mathematics. The use of literature in mathematics instruction enhances students' learning and reasoning by:

■ providing a meaningful context for the mathematics being learned;

■ supporting relevant problem solving;

Figure 5–4 *A kindergarten student counts the tally marks on the class weather chart to show that the weather pictures are in order from most to least.*

▪ integrating mathematics into other disciplines;

▪ relating mathematics to everyday situations; and

▪ engaging students in rich problem solving that strengthens their number sense.

Children's literature easily becomes a springboard for further investigating the concepts or skills embedded in a story. These investigations support reasoning about math that is connected to students' lives and help them understand the relevance of the math they are learning.

Final Thoughts

The process standards—reasoning and proof, problem solving, communication, representation, and connections—are the processes by which students acquire and use the mathematical concepts and skills they are learning. They are interconnected and interdependent on one another. When teaching in the manner that NCTM envisions for our students, we must consider the process standards as well as the content standards when we plan our instructional programs. Reasoning and proof is considered to be one of the most important NCTM standards; however, reasoning relies on the remaining process standards to support its development and effective delivery. Rich problem-solving tasks are the vehicle for promoting the reasoning skills we want our students to develop; communication and representation are how they reveal their rea-

Bill's Coins

Bill's dad gives him fifteen cents for his bank.
Show all of the combinations of coins that Bill can receive.

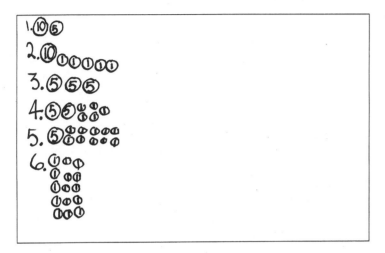

How do you know that you have all of the possible combinations?

I Know I have all of the
combinations because I put the 10 cent's
fisrt 5 cents next and 1 last.

Figure 5–5 *A logical thinking CD task that connects money and number concepts.*

soning to us and others; and the connections they make among mathematical ideas, across other disciplines, and to their everyday lives will support them in reasoning about mathematics in a variety of settings.

Questions for Discussion

1. How do the other process standards help support the reasoning and proof process standard?

2. Reflect on the interconnectedness among the process standards.

3. Which of the remaining process standards (problem solving, communication, representation, and connections) do you feel will be the most challenging for you to implement into your classroom teaching as you help your students develop their reasoning skills? Why do you think so? Discuss with your colleagues a way to overcome this challenge.

6

Assessing Students' Reasoning

"A teacher who continually learns from *children and* about *children can become the most effective assessor of the young child's mathematical understanding."*

—Juanita V. Copley, ed., *Mathematics in the Early Years*

Why Assess Students' Reasoning?

It is important that we know how our students are reasoning. The reasoning they are developing will support them in making sense of the mathematics they are learning. We should make it a priority to unlock the *mysteries* of mathematics for our students by providing them with multiple opportunities to reason about it. Reasoning skills are critical to our students' everyday lives now and in the future. When we encourage our students to share and discuss reasoning, we open a window that presents us with a view of their thinking and understanding about important mathematical ideas and relationships.

Once the window is opened, how do we measure the development of our students' reasoning abilities? It sounds difficult, and in this chapter we share strategies to make assessment of reasoning a manageable task. The first step, and one that is a critical part of the assessment process, is acknowledging assessment as an integral part of your mathematics instruction. When assessment is an ongoing process in your instructional program, it informs and directs the decisions you make for all of your students.

In many of the assessments typically given in schools, the focus is too often on what students do *not* know. Common types of assessments are paper-and-pencil tasks, which generally measure a student's ability to complete a procedure. On this type of an assessment it may be difficult to analyze a student's error if no explanation of thinking or reasoning has been offered. Administering only this type of assessment will give us an incomplete picture of what our students know. While there is a value in administering formal assessments of this kind, we must also make it a goal to continually seek information about our students' progress by using informal assessments. Assessing students' reasoning is difficult when using traditional tests. To better assess how our students are reasoning about mathematics, we can use ongoing formative assessments.

Making assessment a part of our daily instruction gives us a broader method for determining whether students have a deep understanding of the mathematics being taught. When we are assessing students' reasoning, the process does not look different from instruction; rather, it should become a large part of our instruction. Therefore, it is advantageous to focus our assessments on what students know about the mathematics concepts and skills they are learning and how they are reasoning about them.

Formative assessments, which involve authentic contexts in which students are assessed in a variety of situations, effectively measure students' development of reasoning skills. Since young children in the primary grades are learning to become writers, teachers find it difficult to assess with only traditional paper-pencil assessments. What type of assessment process is the most effective in the early childhood years? "It is the process of observing; gathering evidence about a child's knowledge, behaviors, and dispositions; documenting the work that children do and how they do it; and making inferences from that evidence for a variety of purposes" (Copley 2000, 23). Assessments that reveal what young children know and can do include diagnostic interviews, documentation of students' self-monitoring, performance assessment tasks, observations, conversations, writing and picture journals, and portfolios. These assessments are not an interruption in the students' day; rather, students are assessed as they are meaningfully engaged in mathematics.

Students' reasoning is also revealed when they represent and communicate their mathematical thinking, which means that assessment can be an ongoing and integral part of your daily instruction. Opportunities for assessment of reasoning can easily occur in the daily discussions you have with your students. Students' explanations that describe a variety of mathematical ideas and relationships provide you with important information about what they know and understand about the mathematics you are teaching. This chapter explores the usefulness of a variety of formative assessments that can help you assess students' reasoning skills and can be easily implemented into your classroom routine.

Reasoning is a critical thinking skill for our students, but how do we measure our students' ability to reason? Students in grades K-2 who are competent in mathematical reasoning should be able to:

■ use models, known facts, properties, and relationships to explain their reasoning;

■ use patterns and relationships to analyze and explain mathematical situations;

■ justify answers and solutions; and

■ draw logical conclusions about mathematical generalizations and patterns. (NCTM 2003, 29)

We will now explore ways to meaningfully measure the growth of students' reasoning skills.

How to Assess Students' Reasoning

A variety of strategies support the assessment of students' reasoning. These assessment strategies differ from traditional and more formal assessments that involve checking off a correct or incorrect answer. Students in the primary grades are developing as writers, so many of the assessments described in this chapter do not include a student-writing component. Observations and informal conversations with young students provide teachers with critical information about what students know and can do. Many assessments in the primary grades are unplanned yet can provide as much assessment information as those that are planned. The formative assessments recommended can be integrated into daily ongoing instruction and will help you measure the progress of your students' reasoning skills. These assessments use multiple approaches to allow students to show what they know and can do.

We begin by describing the classroom environment that allows you to conduct ongoing assessments. NCTM recommends that teachers create classrooms that are problem-based environments in which students learn mathematics by problem solving. This type of teaching focuses students' learning on mathematical ideas and sense making. In mathematics that is taught traditionally, students tend to focus only on the directions or the procedures that are presented to them rather than on the more meaningful ideas of mathematics. The value of teaching by problem solving has been evident throughout this book in the student dialogues. Students' reasoning abilities in these classrooms were able to grow as they grappled with challenging problems in the different dialogue examples. In a problem-solving classroom, getting the answer and engaging in the thinking and reasoning necessary to problem solve are equally important. (See Figure 6–1.) Problem-solving activities provide a vehicle for you to learn how your students are thinking and reasoning about mathematics. Choosing problem-solving tasks that are relevant to your students will help them see how mathematics connects to their everyday lives.

Teaching mathematics via problem solving can be likened to inquiry-based instruction. This type of instruction supports rich discussions that will enable you to assess how your students are reasoning. The traditional method of direct instruction, in which the teacher presents rules and algorithms for students to memorize, inhibits students' development of reasoning. Teaching mathematics through problem solving provides students with multiple opportunities to investigate the mathematics they are learning. These experiences uncover important ideas and allow students to think more deeply about mathematics concepts and skills. When problem solving becomes the way you teach mathematics, it strongly supports the student discussions that will allow you to informally assess your students daily.

Student Discussions

Informally listening to students during student discussions is crucial for determining their development of reasoning skills. The student dialogues in this book model ways

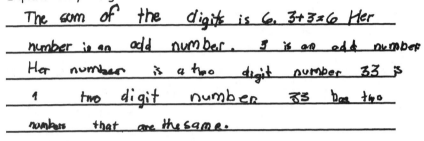

June's Favorite Number

The number on June's house is her favorite number.
Can you figure out June's favorite number?
   Clues:
   •   Her number is a two digit number.
   •   Her two digits are the same.
   •   Her number is an odd number.
   •   The sum of the digits is 6.
What is June's favorite number? __33__

Explain how you figured it out.

The sum of the digits is 6. 3+3=6 Her
number is an odd number. 3 is an odd number
Her number is a two digit number 33 is
a two digit number 33 has two
numbers that are the same.

Figure 6–1 *This student shows an understanding of number concepts in her
written explanation of her reasoning for why 33 is the correct answer.*

for you to assess your students' reasoning skills during discussions. Following are examples of how teachers are able to assess students' ability to reason during their student discussions:

■ *Teachers ask students to explain their reasoning in arriving at a solution to a
problem.* It is important to remember that students may have a correct solution,
but their reasoning in reaching that solution may be flawed. Unless we question
our students about their thinking in solving a problem, a misconception might
not be revealed. Questioning our students provides us with information that can
be used instructionally to redirect students' misconceptions toward reasoning that
makes more sense. Make it a habit to ask all your students to explain their reasoning, which provides you with important assessment information.

■ *Teachers ask students to share their strategies for solving a problem.* After a student shares a strategy and explains the reasoning for the strategy, encourage other
students to share any strategies that may be different. Students will be learning
about a variety of ways to reason about problem solving, and you will be finding
out about students' individual problem-solving strategies and reasoning skills.

■ *Teachers provide students time to work with a partner or in a small group.* When
beginning your student discussions, you may find that some of your students
are hesitant to speak in front of the whole class. However, in smaller groupings

students generally feel less intimidated and are more apt to share their reasoning. Use these opportunities to observe and listen to how your students are thinking and reasoning about a question or task. This is an opportune time to observe students who are not willing to take part in a whole-group discussion.

■ *Teachers often ask students to restate another student's reasoning.* This practice encourages students to listen carefully to their classmates' explanations of reasoning. When asked to restate reasoning, a student must reflect on the reasoning shared in order to restate the thinking in her own words. If the original reasoning is correct but hard to understand, another student's rewording of the reasoning helps to clarify it. Encouraging students to revise flawed reasoning provides the student whose reasoning is flawed an opportunity to reflect and redirect his thinking and reasoning. Additionally, asking the original student to restate his flawed explanation is beneficial because it will help you learn more about how that student is thinking about the mathematics.

The reasoning activities on the CD, and the discussions that follow the completion of these activities, serve easily as informal assessments that will support you in determining the level of your students' reasoning abilities. These activities allow all students to demonstrate their knowledge regardless of where they are in their understandings of the mathematics being taught and how they are reasoning about important mathematical ideas and relationships. The CD activities encourage students to focus on the thinking, reasoning, and processes that are essential for solving problems.

During the discussions you facilitate with your students, it is unlikely that you will be able to assess every student every day. However, before any discussion begins it is helpful to select a small group of students that you want to observe during that day's mathematics discussion. While all students are discussing the mathematics in the activity, make mental notes about the reasoning of the targeted students as well as their understanding of the mathematics in the lesson. These mental notes can then be recorded soon after the discussion as anecdotal notes (e.g., on address labels or index cards). Gather additional data from different targeted groups of students throughout the week.

Observing and Listening to Students

We can learn important information about how our students are reasoning when we observe and listen not only as they work but also when they are involved in mathematical play. When students are working and playing individually or in small groups to complete mathematical tasks, we are presented wonderful opportunities to observe and listen to them. Our observations of our students' interactions with the math they are learning can reveal much about their thinking when we purposefully listen to their explanations of what they are doing. Following are suggestions for how to focus your observations when you are informally assessing students' reasoning. We recommend that you narrow your focus to only one or two of the following suggestions:

■ Can the student explain how he is solving the problem?

■ Is the student's way of solving the problem an appropriate one for the task?

■ If the student's strategy did not work, did the student apply a different strategy?

■ Does the student make any connections to mathematical ideas learned previously?

■ Is the student able to self-monitor her thinking and reasoning?

■ Does the student's representation accurately convey the reasoning used in thinking about the task?

Record observational data immediately following any planned observation. Many teachers do this by attaching an index card for each child on a clipboard or by entering students' information into a class grid. It is important to consider that relying only on observations can limit the information we gather about our students. The assessment data collected might only be an interpretation of what was observed. However, when a conversation accompanies the observation, whether planned or unplanned, additional evidence is provided to help make instructional decisions.

CLASSROOM-TESTED TIP

If you are asking your students to work on tasks in small groups or with a partner, this is an excellent time to informally observe students to assess their understanding of concepts and reasoning skills. Record observational notes as students work and interact together and as you listen to them discuss a problem or task. Ask students probing questions to gather additional information about how they are reasoning as they complete the tasks. As we mentioned earlier, students who are hesitant to share their thinking in a large-group setting will be more likely to share their reasoning in a small-group situation that is less intimidating. Think about which students you want to collect data from during that day's mathematics lesson and then record this information discreetly. You may be recording data from only one small group during a lesson, but it is important to visit all the groups as they are problem solving.

Conversations

While whole-group student discussions are conversations that are planned, the informal conversations you have with your students can also provide you with information about their reasoning abilities. Whether students are engaged in mathematical play, at centers, working individually, in a small group, or with a partner, these are times when you can observe and ask questions about what they are thinking and doing.

CLASSROOM-TESTED TIP

Following are several questions or prompts you can implement into your informal conversations with students to promote mathematical thinking and reasoning:

- Why do you think your answer is right?

- How did you figure out your answer?

- Could you solve this problem differently?

- Tell me about what you did.

- How did you decide to solve the problem that way?

- What will you do next?

- How can you check to see if you have a close estimate?

- Tell me more about what you did in this task.

Written Responses

Students' written responses provide us with a valuable source of information about their development of reasoning. Written responses provide visual evidence of how students are reasoning about the mathematical concepts and skills we are teaching. Your analysis of these responses will help you make decisions about your mathematics program and instruction. In addition, written responses provide concrete evidence of students' learning that can help parents to see how their child is reasoning about mathematics and to appreciate the child's progress in understanding the concepts and skills being taught.

Sometimes it can be helpful to ask students to share their written responses with their classmates. Students' sharing of their problem-solving strategies and reasoning enables others to hear a variety of ways to think. When other strategies are described, encourage students to test the strategies on additional problems. This is similar to asking students to restate another student's reasoning during a discussion. Students will be discovering important ideas about different strategies that can lead to generalizations. The sharing of written responses provides you with another opportunity to assess students' reasoning skills.

Very young students who are beginning to develop writing skills can dictate how they are thinking about mathematical ideas. These dictations become a classroom record of a variety of mathematics topics that students are learning. Recordings can be from individual students or from the entire class. Students who are not yet writing can record their thinking in picture journals instead of the traditional writing journals.

Representations

Students' representations are another form of informal assessment that allows us to understand more about their reasoning abilities. Students' concrete, pictorial, and/or symbolic representations show us how they are organizing and communicating their thinking and reasoning. (See Figure 6–2.) Observing how students utilize these representations of mathematical ideas and relationships provides us with valuable information. To make sense of the mathematics they are learning, students will need to reason about the mathematics in order to represent it. Students' representations aid them in visualizing generalizations and conjectures they have made, such as a student who is recording patterns on a 1–100 chart to help in making a generalization about those patterns.

Diagnostic Interviews

Diagnostic interviews are an effective method for gathering data about students' ability to reason. A diagnostic interview is a brief one-on-one discussion with a student that helps you identify how a student is reasoning about a specific mathematics concept or skill as well as any strategies the student is using in the reasoning process. Many teachers find it manageable to schedule several interviews daily while other students are working independently on a task or at centers. Generally, five minutes is ample time to obtain the assessment information needed from a student. When you allow yourself time to do a diagnostic interview with a student, you are more likely to identify the misconceptions or difficulties he may be experiencing with the mathematics he is learning. The reasoning students share during an interview helps to demonstrate the depth of their understanding about a concept or skill. In addition, these interviews provide information that can help you plan instruction to meet the needs of all your students.

CLASSROOM-TESTED TIP

When planning to do a diagnostic interview, prepare the questions and materials ahead of time. Begin an interview with a quick warm-up, a task that the student is able to do with success. Then ask the student questions that will provide evidence of his ability to reason. Many of the questions you will want to ask are those provided in Chapters 1, 3, and 4. Also, the questions modeled throughout the student dialogues will be helpful to use during an interview assessment. A diagnostic interview is not a time to teach; rather, it is a time to observe and listen to what students know and are able to do, and how they are reasoning about important mathematical ideas and relationships. It is essential that you remain neutral in your responses. At first this may be difficult for students to accept if they are used to a different type of response such as "Great!" or "Way to go!" Smiles, frowns, or other positive or negative responses will cause students to think that the answer they gave is right or wrong. And, of course, allowing sufficient wait time during any interview is extremely important.

Where does the 40 belong?

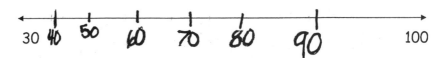

Estimate where the number 40 belongs on the number line.

Explain your thinking.

It is closer to 30 because 40 is only 10 away from 30 and 100 is 60 away from 40 away. And 30 is closer to 40 than 100.

Where does the 40 belong?

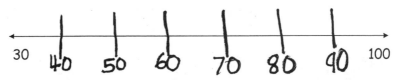

Estimate where the number 40 belongs on the number line.

Explain your thinking.

I used two of my fingers to mak a margine and I went all the way to the end without trying to move my fingers, so it would be a close estimatoin.

Figure 6–2 *These student examples show understanding of the task in different ways although the placement of numbers is off in the top example.*

Another effective strategy for assessing reasoning is to ask questions that are open-ended. These questions encourage students to reason more thoughtfully because they are not as tightly defined as traditional questions, which usually generate one right answer. Open-ended questions can be answered using a variety of methods or can have many right answers. Consider the cupcakes and brownies problem in Chapter 1. In this problem, students were asked to think about various ways that the teacher might send ten cupcakes and brownies to her brother for his birthday. This question encouraged students to find multiple combinations for ten as they explored the part-part-whole relationship of number. In students' explanations and justifications for how they knew they had found all the possible combinations, the teacher was able to informally assess how students were thinking and what strategies they were using to solve the task.

An open-ended question about the computation of a problem also supports students' reasoning. Simply asking students to mentally compute $36 - 9$ can stimulate considerable discussion about the different ways students solve this problem. It is likely some students may solve it mentally using a traditional algorithm; however, other students may describe strategies that require manipulation of numbers. Consider this explanation from a grade 2 student:

It's 27. The problem is 36 minus 9. I know that 36 minus 6 is 30. That's easy. But we had to minus 9 so 3 more needs to be taken away because 6 and 3 is nine. So I just counted back from 30 three times. 29, 28, 27. 36 minus 9 is 27.

In listening to this explanation, a teacher would know that the student was comfortable in manipulating numbers in a nontraditional way. This student has a strong sense of numbers and can think flexibly about these numbers, which will support her in reasoning later about operations. When we expect our students to justify why a specific strategy is useful in solving a problem, their reasoning becomes available to us and other students. One student's reasoning about solving a problem may make more sense to another student than the traditional algorithm. As students share their different strategies for solving problems, much can be learned about how students are thinking and reasoning about mathematics.

A constructed-response question is a type of question that requires students to apply what they know about a mathematics concept or skill to explain why the solution makes sense or is valid. For example, the first part of a constructed-response question may ask students to estimate two sums, and the second part of the question then prompts students to use what they know about estimation to explain why their solution makes sense. This information is typically represented using words, numbers, or pictures. The answer to the last part of the question provides valuable information about a student's understanding of the mathematical concept in the first part. (See Figure 6–3.)

Performance assessment tasks are generally open-ended as well and require more thinking and reasoning than a traditional assessment. They reveal what a student knows and can do as well as his abilities to communicate mathematically. When

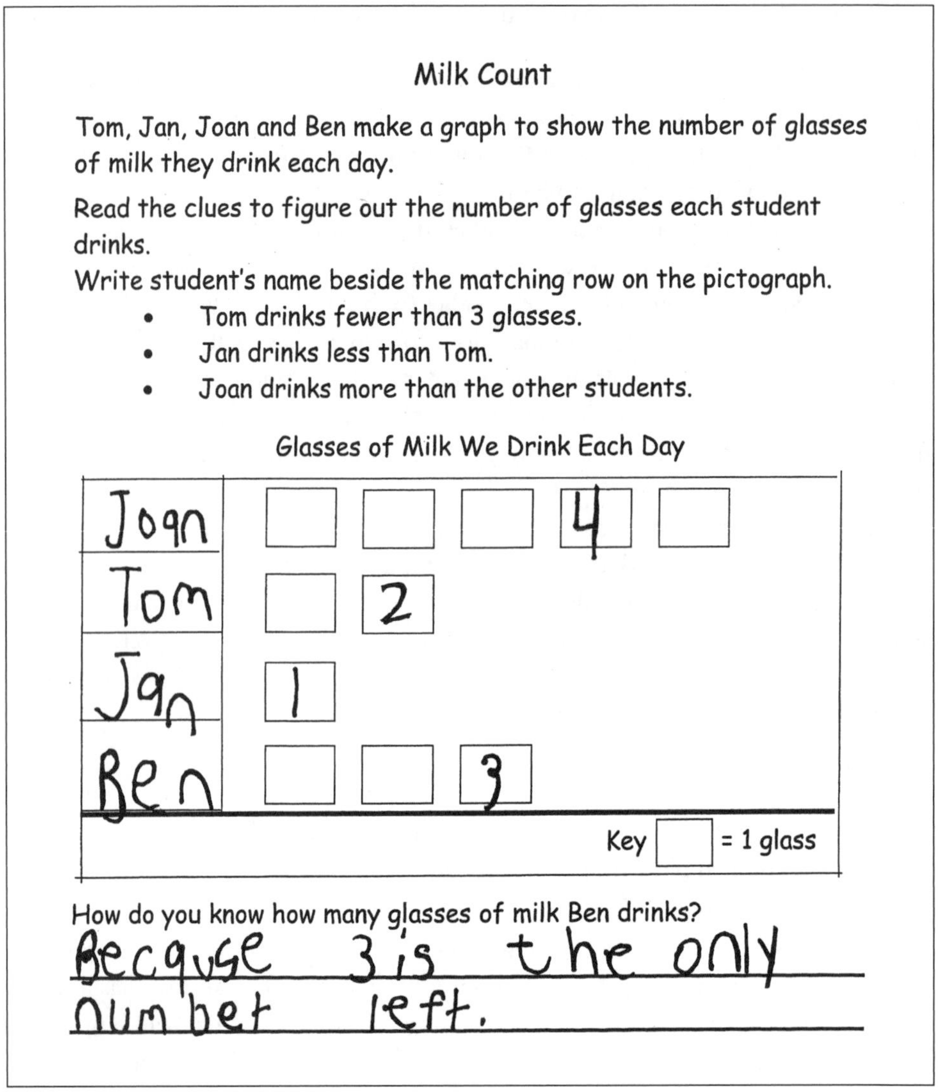

Milk Count

Tom, Jan, Joan and Ben make a graph to show the number of glasses of milk they drink each day.

Read the clues to figure out the number of glasses each student drinks.

Write student's name beside the matching row on the pictograph.

- Tom drinks fewer than 3 glasses.
- Jan drinks less than Tom.
- Joan drinks more than the other students.

Glasses of Milk We Drink Each Day

Joan	☐	☐	☐	4	☐
Tom	☐	2			
Jan	1				
Ben	☐	☐	3		

Key ☐ = 1 glass

How do you know how many glasses of milk Ben drinks?

Because 3 is the only number left.

Figure 6–3 *Although the student's final answer is correct, an error has been made in Joan's data. This allowed the teacher to see some misunderstanding in the student's problem solving.*

providing open-ended tasks of this nature, we are able to accommodate the varied learning styles of our students. Students are encouraged to solve problems in a way that makes sense to them. When administering a performance assessment task to pairs of students, you can observe what students say to each other as they work on the task together. These tasks involve the manipulation of materials for students to make decisions and reason about the task. Students are actively participating in this type of assessment.

It is critical that we support primary students in beginning to develop the skills needed to assess their own learning. This process of self-evaluating helps students assume responsibility for their own learning. Helping students to learn how to monitor the progress of what they are learning and how they are reasoning about mathematics can begin in the primary years. Many of the student dialogues demonstrate ways that students can self-evaluate. We can model self-monitoring for our students by asking questions such as, "I wonder if I have answered every part of the question?" In addition, a simple rubric that encourages students to reflect on their reasoning is included on the CD.

CLASSROOM-TESTED TIP

To help students develop self-monitoring skills, or the ability to reflect on their thinking and reasoning, encourage them to ask themselves questions such as the following when they are investigating problems and tasks:

- What do I know about this problem?

- What strategy or strategies will help me?

- What do I think the answer will be, and why do I think this?

- Where should I begin?

- Do I need to revise my reasoning?

- Will the explanation of my reasoning be clear to others?

- Am I done?

The closure of a lesson provides you with another way to assess students' learning and to see if they are making sense of mathematics. This is a time for students to share what they have learned in that day's lesson, and our role is simply to be the facilitator of this brief discussion. Allowing students to summarize their learning in a student discussion provides you with an informal assessment of what they know and can do regarding the mathematics learned in the day's lesson. If students have any misconceptions, they are often revealed during the closure of a lesson. These errors in thinking can be noted and clarified so that students are not leaving with confused understandings.

Exit cards are a quick snapshot of students' reasoning and are easily implemented into a lesson. They are given to students at the conclusion of a lesson; however, exit cards should not be confused with the closure that was just described. Exit cards differ from closure in that these cards are individually completed by students and do not involve a group discussion. They are easy to prepare by recording a question that requires students to reason about an idea or a relationship investigated in that day's lesson.

Finally, portfolios are a collection of student work over a period of time. Work included in an assessment portfolio is selected by the student and the teacher. These folders become a history of a student's growth and show the many ways in which the student is thinking mathematically. Teachers often include observational notes, results of diagnostic interviews, and anecdotal notes from informal conversations in students' portfolios. Encourage older primary students to reflect on the work that is included in a portfolio, which is another form of self-assessment. Portfolios are concrete evidence of progress that can be shared with students' families.

Any of the information we collect about our students' learning should be useful data that enables us to make sound instructional decisions for our students. We must be able to interpret assessment information from a variety of sources so that we are able to measure how students are reasoning in different ways. The data we collect also presents us with information about our teaching. Our reflections help us decide if our teaching and delivery are meeting the needs of all of our students. When we consistently infuse formative assessments into our daily teaching, they will guide the instructional decisions we make for all of our students.

Development of Students' Reasoning Skills

Students may demonstrate the following characteristics as they develop reasoning skills. These descriptors are meant to be general observations about students' development of reasoning.*

- Students with undeveloped reasoning abilities provide little or no evidence of a strategy or way of reasoning about a problem. If they do describe a strategy or explain their reasoning, it does not help them reach a solution that makes sense. They have difficulty understanding the reasoning of others.

- Students who are beginning to develop reasoning skills are implementing strategies and reasoning skills that are partially developed; however, the strategies or reasoning they are using do not support them in arriving at a fully developed solution.

- When students' reasoning becomes more developed, they begin to use a strategy and reasoning that guide them to a correct solution; however, they do not attempt to apply multiple strategies to arrive at the same solution. Students' reasoning about an idea or relationship is based on one or a few examples, although supporting the generalization is difficult.

- Students whose reasoning is stronger are comfortable applying several strategies to reach a solution, and they understand which strategies are more efficient than others for solving and reasoning about a problem. They are beginning to under-

---

*These descriptors were adapted from the work of Bena Kallick and Ross Brewer in *How to Assess Problem-Solving Skills in Math* (1997, 125).

stand that a generalization, or conjecture, should be justified with multiple examples, and they are able to develop informal mathematical arguments to do this.

■ Students who are efficient and more creative in their development of multiple strategies also have different ways to reason about mathematical ideas and relationships. They are able to self-evaluate their reasoning for the purpose of refining it, and they evaluate others' reasoning in an attempt to make sense of the mathematics they are learning. Students are able to make conjectures and develop mathematical arguments about more complex ideas.

Assessing Students' Reasoning with Rubrics

A rubric is an assessment tool commonly used by teachers. It generally consists of a scale of three to five points and is used to rate a student's performance. A three-point rubric is sufficient for assessing a student's reasoning. Following is a sample of a general rubric for assessing reasoning:

3   Student states reasoning that is clear and makes sense to others. The reasoning is well developed with several examples of justification.

2   Student states reasoning that makes sense; however, it is supported by only one or two examples of justification. Or student may have a flaw in the reasoning but upon reflecting on the reasoning is able to revise the original thinking.

1   Student is unable to explain why a solution is correct. Or student has a flaw in reasoning, and in reflecting upon it, is unable to revise the original thinking.

In Chapter 1, we discussed the importance of explaining to students the expectations you will have for them in communicating their reasoning. Just as it is important for students to understand why they will be expected to discuss, write, or represent their reasoning, it is also essential that they understand how you will be assessing their development of reasoning throughout the school year. A general rubric may be sufficient initially for your assessment needs and certainly easier for older primary students to understand. However, you may later decide that a more specific rubric is necessary to assess your students' progress in explaining justifications and developing informal mathematical arguments. These informal assessments of students' reasoning skills can guide you in determining how to best meet your students' needs. Assessing students' progress in their ability to explain mathematical ideas, state conjectures, provide justifications and make informal mathematical arguments will help you plan next steps to provide additional experiences to support their reasoning skills. These experiences build the foundational skills necessary for students' more formal reasoning in later school years. When we ask our students to reflect on their reasoning, it not only assists us in understanding how they are thinking but also allows them to self-evaluate their reasoning and evaluate the reasoning of their classmates.

Final Thoughts

Students in prekindergarten through grade 2 are developing their ability to explain their reasoning. It is essential that we understand how our students are thinking about the mathematics they are learning so we can plan instruction that enhances their reasoning abilities. Assessment must then become an integral and ongoing part of our mathematics teaching so that we are able to monitor our students' growth in reasoning and make instructional decisions that will affect all our students in positive ways.

The most efficient assessments are often those that can be done easily and informally. The discussions you have with your students will provide you with daily opportunities to monitor their development as mathematical thinkers. Students' written responses and representations will give you visible evidence of how they are reasoning that you can then share with their families. Planned and unplanned observations and conversations are absolutely a must with young learners. Utilizing multiple types of assessment throughout our daily instruction allow us to understand more about our students' thought processes and the depth of understanding they have about mathematics concepts and skills. In addition, we cannot overlook the importance of supporting our students in learning how to self-monitor their reasoning as well as evaluate the reasoning of others. When students are provided these experiences, they will take ownership of their learning, which will support them in becoming powerful mathematical thinkers.

Questions for Discussion

1. The importance of assessing students' reasoning skills was the focus of this chapter. A variety of ways to do this were discussed. Which of these recommendations will you feel the most comfortable using? Why do you feel this way?

2. Which method of assessment are you the most uncomfortable using? Reflect on ways to reduce your discomfort, or discuss with your colleagues possible ways to make the assessment process more manageable for you and your students.

3. Suppose you have observed that several of your students are experiencing difficulties in making conjectures that are clearly developed and understood. What types of activities would you plan to help these students strengthen this reasoning skill?

CHAPTER 7

Reasoning and Proof Across the Content Standards

Effective teaching conveys a belief that each student can and is expected to understand mathematics and that each will be supported in his or her efforts to accomplish this goal.

—National Council of Teachers of Mathematics, *Principles and Standards for School Mathematics*

We have been focusing on how to help students develop the process skill of reasoning and proof and on how students' ability to reason supports their sense making of mathematics concepts and skills. The interconnectedness of reasoning and proof with all of the process standards is critical in supporting students' reasoning skills. Students communicate their reasoning in student discussions, in written responses, and through representations. Students' ability to communicate reasoning in a variety of ways allows them to become flexible as well as reflective thinkers. As they reflect on their reasoning and the understandings they are developing about mathematics, their reasoning and conceptual understandings are refined and internalized.

In addition to talking about their reasoning, it is beneficial for students to represent their reasoning concretely, pictorially, and symbolically. These representations assist them in understanding their thinking and reasoning about a mathematical idea or relationship. For the teacher, student representations become tools that reveal misconceptions about a student's reasoning when they occur. The connections that students make among mathematical ideas support them in developing deeper understandings about each idea. Not only do students strengthen their reasoning skills as they make connections among mathematical ideas, but when they reason about mathematical ideas connected to real-world situations, their reasoning is applied in practical ways. Connecting mathematics to other disciplines in your instructional program is another example of students' application of the math they are learning. You will observe how the reasoning and proof process standard interconnects with the other process standards, as well as the content standards, in the student dialogues presented in this chapter.

In Chapter 5, we discussed how the process standards overlap, and this is also true about the connections among process standards and content standards. Mathematics is considered to be an abstract discipline, and students' application of the process standard of reasoning and proof allows them to make sense of mathematics. As students solve problems that are interesting and challenging, they naturally use intuitive, inductive, and deductive reasoning skills to think about a variety of problem-solving situations. Teaching mathematics through the process of problem solving provides our students with multiple opportunities to reason, propose conjectures, and create mathematical arguments. In order for students to make this reasoning explicit, they must use the process standards of communication and representation. Students' ability to connect the mathematics they are learning to other mathematical ideas, across all disciplines, and in their everyday lives allows them to reason in a variety of settings that demonstrate application of mathematical ideas.

The National Council of Teachers of Mathematics (2000) has outlined the content standards for elementary students and has organized those standards in five content areas: number and operations, algebra, measurement, geometry, and data analysis and probability. While we focus on helping students to develop critical understandings of this content, we must also support our students in developing their process skills of reasoning and proof, problem solving, communication, representation, and connections. This chapter provides examples of student dialogues and activities that illustrate how the content and process standards are intertwined. The student dialogues demonstrate how students are reasoning about the various mathematical ideas and relationships presented. The activities discussed in the dialogues are aligned to the NCTM standards and expectations for students in prekindergarten through grade 2 (NCTM 2000). Additional resources to support you in implementing these activities are available on the CD.

Number and Operations

In prekindergarten through grade 2, students strengthen their number sense with numbers from zero to twenty and explore the operations of addition and subtraction. Students who have a good sense of number think intuitively about numbers and their relationships. Number sense develops over time with a variety of experiences in which students are reasoning about number ideas and relationships. These experiences include those in which students are exploring numbers, visualizing them in different ways, and relating numbers in other ways besides the limitations of traditional algorithms.

In the early years of this grade band, students are developing understanding about number through counting activities, and they are moving beyond the procedural task of rote counting. "The *meaning* attached to counting is the key conceptual idea on which all other number concepts are developed" (Van de Walle and Lovin 2006, 39). Provide students with multiple opportunities to count concrete objects and to play board games in which counting or comparing is involved. These activities encourage students' use of one-to-one correspondence—that is, their understanding that for each item counted there is one and only one number name. An early understanding about number is that of the cardinality principle. When students have finished counting a set of objects we can help them develop this understanding by asking often, "How many?" Students who recount the objects in the set have not developed the idea that the last number counted also represents the total quantity in the set.

Primary students are beginning to develop their ability to count on and count back from different numbers such as counting on from eleven or counting back from nine. When students practice this counting strategy with counters or in a game format, students begin to see the usefulness of this strategy. It eventually becomes a meaningful counting strategy to use in addition and subtraction situations.

In Chapter 3, we discussed the importance of giving students opportunities to reason about number relationships. Additional number relationships we will want students to reason about include the following:

- Spatial relationships—Provide students opportunities to use dice and dominoes in game situations, which helps them to recognize quantities without counting.

- One and two more, one and two less—This activity involves more than counting on 1 or 2. It encompasses the student's ability to describe five as being one less than six or one more than four. Expect students to describe a number in a variety of ways.

- Benchmarks of 5 and 10—In the early grades, students benefit from using counting tools such as a 5-frame and a 10-frame. These tools are included in the CD for your students' use.

- Part-part-whole relationships—To conceptualize a whole as being made up of two or more parts is the most important relationship about number that is developed by young children. The student dialogue in Chapter 1 demonstrated how students were reasoning about the part-part-whole relationship in the cupcakes and brownies task.

CLASSROOM-TESTED TIP

It is recommended that you begin with a 5-frame before introducing a 10-frame to students. A 5-frame is a row of connected boxes that focuses on relationships to 5. Once students are familiar with a 5-frame, introduce them to a 10-frame, which is a 2×5 array of boxes in which counters are placed to represent numbers through 10. Beginning at the left of a 10-frame, students fill the top row first. When the top row is filled, counters are placed in the bottom row, again beginning at the left. Observing students as they represent numbers on a 10-frame allows you to assess students' number concept development. Consider the following example: A student with eight counters on a 10-frame is asked to next show six counters. If the student takes away two, he may have counted back or known that six and two are eight. If the student removes all the counters and starts over, he may see numbers as unrelated and does not recognize that he can use number relationships to create a more efficient strategy to make the new number. Of course, it is always important to ask students how they make each new number. This reveals more about how a student is thinking and reasoning.

Young children benefit greatly when they are allowed many opportunities to build understandings about the part-part-whole relationship. These experiences typically begin in kindergarten and extend into grade 1 and help students develop fluency of number combinations to 10 as well as foundational understandings for the operations of addition and subtraction. The part-part-whole relationship is foundational for many mathematical concepts that students will develop in later grades such as place value, missing addends, fractions, composing and decomposing shapes (a hexagonal pattern block can be composed of six triangular pattern blocks, three rhombi, or two trapezoids), and measurement (number of minutes in a quarter hour, number of inch units in a foot) to name a few.

Students in prekindergarten through grade 2 are developing the relationship of more and less. Prekindergarten students intuitively understand the concept of more, but the idea of less is more abstract. To help students with the concept of less, make it a habit to pair the word *less* with the word *more* For example, ask young students the following two questions when they are comparing two sets of objects: "Which is more?" and "Which is less?" Expect them to also explain how they know which set is more and which set is less.

Primary students are developing understandings about numbers to 100 and are becoming familiar with the counting patterns on a 100-chart. In Chapter 2, we shared a student dialogue, "Guess My Number," which demonstrated the usefulness of a 100-chart as a tool to support students' reasoning skills.

Students in grade 1 and 2 are beginning to learn that addition and subtraction are inverse operations. They are capable of solving problems that are more complex than join and separate problems. An example of a traditional problem is this one: *Ten birds are on a branch. Three fly away. How many birds are left?* Here is an example of a more challenging problem for students to solve: *Nick has a total of twelve cars. Some are blue and five are green. How many cars are blue?* This particular problem requires an understanding of the part-part-whole relationship for twelve and also uses the algebraic language of *some*. Rewording a problem in this manner encourages students to reason in order to solve it.

Students are learning to take apart and combine numbers in a variety of ways as well as explain strategies that are useful and efficient in problem solving when traditional algorithms are not yet understood. By the end of grade 2, students have developed quick recall of addition facts and related subtraction facts and are developing fluency of multi-digit addition and subtraction.

The following questions and prompts are effective in promoting students' reasoning about number relationships and computation:

■ How do you know?

■ What is a different way to show this number?

■ What numbers come between 22 and 30? Why does it not include the number 22?

■ Do you think there are more than 15 in this set? How do you know?

■ Explain how you thought about this problem in order to solve it.

■ Could you do that with different numbers?

■ Draw a picture to show how you were thinking about this problem.

■ When I say "12," what do you think about?

■ The total is 20. What could be the parts that make up the total?

■ How can 55 be shown in different ways?

■ What are three different ways to make 25¢ using pennies, nickels, and dimes?

■ Explain two different ways to compute 33 – 19.

Students in the primary grades are developing understandings about properties of number such as the commutative property of addition (the sum stays the same when the order of the addends is changed), the identity property of addition (adding zero to a number gives a sum identical to the given number), and the inverse operation of addition and subtraction. In Chapters 3 and 4, student dialogues demonstrated how they were reasoning about the commutative and identity properties of addition. Students were conjecturing about the operations and providing informal justifications for why the conjectures were always true.

Place value is an important focus in this grade band. In kindergarten and grade 1, students begin this process by thinking about groups of ten items as a unit. Students in grade 2 connect these understandings to our place-value system of numeration. It is important for young students to understand that ten items can be perceived as one entity and that several sets of ten as well as single units can be counted to represent larger quantities. Young children are also learning that the digit positions in a number determine what it represents and that there are patterns in how numbers are formed. Just as it is important for students to represent smaller numbers in a variety of ways, it is crucial that students represent larger numbers in different ways. For example, 150 can be represented as 1 hundred and 5 tens; 15 tens; or 10 tens and 50 ones. When students engage in these experiences, it helps them reason about computation of larger numbers.

The importance of reasoning in developing students' deeper understandings about mathematics concepts and skills has been stressed throughout this book. These understandings are further developed when learning is supported by the remaining process standards of problem solving, communication, representation, and connections. In this chapter, we provide student dialogues for each of the content standards to illustrate how reasoning and proof enhances the ideas and relationships in that content. As you read through the dialogues, notice how the other process standards and/or content standards are integrated in a lesson's activity.

Lesson: Which Is Larger? $\frac{1}{4}$ or $\frac{1}{2}$?

The following dialogue in a grade 1 classroom was related to the number content standard, specifically fractions. The teacher shared this scenario with his students:

*Pretend you will share a pizza with a grown-up in your family.
Draw a picture to show how you will share the pizza so each of you have the same amount.*

After students completed their drawings, the teacher allowed several students time to describe their pizzas. The teacher facilitated the following discussion, which enabled him to informally assess students' developing understandings about fractional concepts:

TEACHER: Tell me something about the pizza you drew.
STUDENT: On my pizza, I made a different kind for my mom. I have pepperoni, and my mom likes veggie.
TEACHER: What part of the pizza is for you?
STUDENT: I get this half of the pizza.
TEACHER: I see. You get one-half of the pizza. What does your mom get?
STUDENT: She gets the other half!
TEACHER: Your drawing shows you get one-half and your mom gets one-half of the pizza. Could we show what you and your mom get in another way?
STUDENT: Oh, yeah. My brother showed me. It's with a two on the bottom and a one on top.
TEACHER: Show me how you write one-half. *(Student writes one-half symbolically.)* I'd like you to make another pizza. *(Teacher draws a circle on the board.)* Think about how you would share this pretend pizza with three other people so you each have the same amount. *(Students are given time to think.)*
STUDENT: I can cut it like this. *(Student draws three vertical lines on the circle.)*
TEACHER: Explain what you did.

STUDENT: I have four parts of the pizza now. Three parts for my friends, and one part for me.

TEACHER: What do the rest of you think?

STUDENT: She's right about the four pieces. But some of the pieces are more so they can't have the same. I wouldn't like it if I got the small piece!

STUDENT: We can cut the pizza another way.

TEACHER: Show us what you were thinking. *(Student draws two intersecting lines on another circle on the board. The lines divide the circle into four equal parts.)* The parts look equal, but how do you know for sure?

STUDENT: You could draw it on paper and cut it out. Then put the parts on each other, and if no parts stick out they're equal.

TEACHER: *(The teacher gives students time to draw a representation of a pizza divided into fourths.)* Who would like to describe how they made their pizza? *(Several students again share.)*

STUDENT: My pizza is cheese for me, pepperoni for my dad, veggie for my mom, and fruit for my sister.

TEACHER: So how much of the pizza will you each get?

STUDENT: We each get one piece of the pizza. We get fours. Wait, we all get one-fourth.

TEACHER: What do you mean?

STUDENT: Well, there're four pieces in the pizza, and they're all the same size. We each get one of the four pieces. So that's one-fourth. The parts have to be even if we share them.

TEACHER: So fractional parts need to be equal parts? *(Students agree.)*

The teacher revisited the pizza task the next day. His focus was to observe how students were reasoning about the sizes of one-half and one-fourth.

TEACHER: Yesterday you made pizzas and showed halves and fourths. Which do you think is more? One-fourth or one-half? Work with a partner to answer this. You may draw pictures to help you. *(Students are given fifteen minutes to work together.)*

TEACHER: What do you think? Is one-fourth more? Or is one-half more?

STUDENT: One-fourth is more. *(At least four other students agreed.)*

TEACHER: How do you know?

STUDENT: This is one-half *(pointing to one-half of a circle)* and this is . . . *(student pauses)* Can I change my mind?

TEACHER: Why do you want to change your thinking?

STUDENT: Because I think one-half is bigger than one-fourth. You have to have a real big pizza so the four pieces are more than the two pieces.

TEACHER: Tell us more about what you are thinking.

STUDENT: Well, you could have one of the four pieces be bigger than the one-half. *(Many students are puzzled.)* Here are my pizzas. *(See Figure 7–1.)*

TEACHER: Oh, I see. In the way that you drew them, one-fourth of the first pizza is larger than one-half of the second pizza. What if both pizzas are the same size?

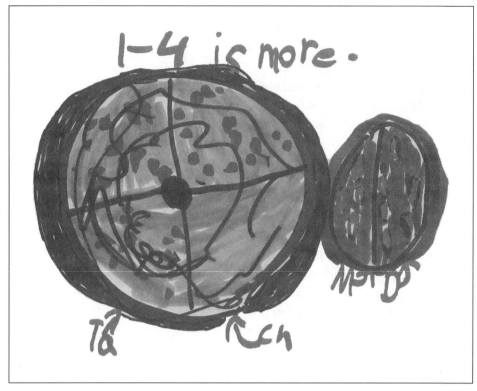

Figure 7–1 *A student's representation showed that one-fourth was larger than one-half, which revealed flawed reasoning because she drew pizzas of different sizes to compare the fractions.*

STUDENT: Can I draw them again and show you? *(The teacher labels the chart paper and the student draws two circles the same size on chart paper. See Figure 7–2.)*

TEACHER: What does everyone think?

STUDENT: One-half is bigger if both are the same size!

STUDENT: But one-fourth has a four in it, and one-half just has a two in it.

STUDENT: The one-half part is a bigger piece *(pointing to the drawing)* and the other one is a littler cut *(pointing to the drawing divided into fourths).*

TEACHER: *(To another student)*, explain to us what *(student)* just said.

STUDENT: He said when a shape is cut more, then the pieces are going to be smaller.

STUDENT: Yeah, you cut and cut and the pieces get more but smaller.

TEACHER: What if I cut the pizza into one hundred pieces? Would you rather have one-hundredths of a pizza or one-half? *(Students all agree on one-half.)*

STUDENT: If you take one piece out of one hundred, you'll have teeny tiny pieces like a mouse piece.

TEACHER: Which is more? One-fourth or one-half?

STUDENT: One-half!

TEACHER: In your math journal, explain how you know one-half is more than one-fourth. You can use drawings and numbers in your explanation.

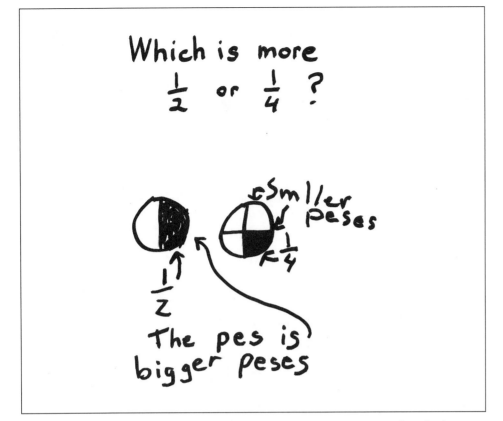

Figure 7-2 *The teacher allowed the student in Figure 7–1 to revise her thinking. This drawing showed a better understanding of which fraction was larger.*

This discussion supported students' reasoning about fractional parts. Students were strengthening their number sense as they discussed which fractional part was larger, one-fourth or one-half. The teacher connected their informal knowledge to more formal language when he modeled the specific names for fractional parts, which students were learning to represent symbolically. Students' understanding of the part-part-whole relationship was necessary because a fraction's name tells how many parts of that size are necessary to make the whole. One student's reasoning about the comparison of one-fourth and one-half in her different-sized pizzas demonstrated the importance of comparing two wholes of the same size. Students also stated a generalization about fractions when they noticed that when more fractional parts were used to make the whole, the parts became smaller.

Reasoning occurs naturally throughout the number and operations content standard. In Chapter 3, we discussed the ideas and relationships about number that were important for students to reason about. Several of these are listed below:

- Number properties—Commutative and identity properties were explored in several of the student dialogues.

■ Invented procedures—Students' creation of procedures that are not bound by traditional algorithms should be justified for why the procedure works and whether it works with other numbers.

■ Outcomes of calculations—It is important for students to generate reasoning about their exploration of how quantities are related to one another, which helps them make sense of the calculations.

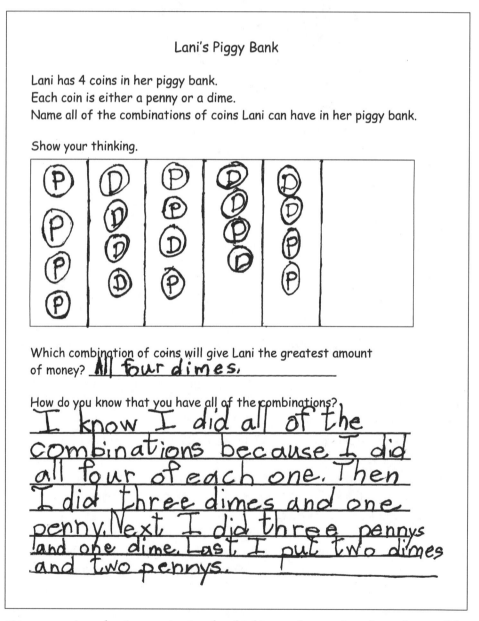

Figure 7-3 *A student's organization for thinking and reasoning about the possible combinations of coins Lani could have in her piggy bank.*

Many of the CD activities focus on the number and operations content standard to help you provide your students with a variety of reasoning experiences. As we have emphasized previously, the discussions that occur during or following the completion of any activity help to solidify the understandings students are developing. When students make their reasoning about number and operations visible in daily student discussions, in written responses, or in representations, they will be strengthening their reasoning skills. (See Figure 7–3.)

Algebra

NCTM recommends that the content of algebra be taught in all grades, from prekindergarten through grade 12. We must provide our students with many opportunities to reason algebraically throughout the school year. These experiences help to build a firm foundation of understanding that will prepare students for more complex thinking in algebra in middle school and high school. "Rather than the algebra you may remember from your high school days, the algebra intended for K–8 focuses on patterns, relationships and functions, and the use of various representations—symbolic, numeric, and graphic—to help make sense of all sorts of mathematical situations" (Van de Walle and Lovin 2006, 290).

By providing multiple experiences in which young students are engaged in reasoning about a variety of algebraic concepts, we are helping them develop the foundational ideas needed to successfully understand higher-level algebraic thinking and reasoning. Students' early algebraic experiences typically begin in prekindergarten as they reason about patterning. In kindergarten, students continue their explorations of patterns and are beginning to understand that a part or *unit* of a pattern consistently repeats, which they later understand as the core of the pattern. In grades 1 and 2, students are also reasoning about numeric patterns and are beginning to understand that growing patterns change from one value to another in a predictable manner. Patterning is the foundation that reinforces and strengthens one's ability to see relationships, to solve problems, and to make generalizations.

CLASSROOM-TESTED TIP

Below are some questions and prompts that you can use to promote students' reasoning about algebraic concepts:

- How are these shapes alike? How are the shapes different?

- Tell what part of the pattern is repeating. How do you know?

- What shape would appear next?

- Use what you know about the pattern unit and predict what shape will be last in the pattern.

■ Use what you know about the pattern unit and predict what the tenth shape will be in the pattern. How did you decide?

■ How could we make this pattern in a different way?

■ How would the pattern change if we changed the _____ to a _____?

■ Describe how the pattern is changing (growth pattern).

In addition to repeating and growing patterns, primary students understand other types of patterns such as the following:

■ expanding patterns found in songs and literature

■ patterns from nature

■ man-made patterns

■ patterns in literature

■ patterns in behavior and routines

■ patterns in time (e.g., lunch is always after math class)

CLASSROOM-TESTED TIP

To help students develop their ability to reason algebraically, provide experiences that allow them to practice the following skills:

■ reason about balance in equations;

■ solve problems in a variety of ways;

■ represent mathematical ideas and relationships in a variety of ways, including symbolically (see Figure 7–4);

■ reason about functional relationships such as those described in the student dialogue in Chapter 2 (see Figure 7–5);

■ use inductive and deductive reasoning;

■ work with variables such as using symbols that describe a relationship between two quantities, represent an unknown quantity, or represent mathematical properties in a proposed conjecture such as the commutative property ($a + b = b + a$);

■ use models (objects, pictures, or symbols) to represent understanding of quantitative relationships such as addition and subtraction; and

■ describe qualitative change such as the growth in students' heights and quantitative changes such as a flower's growth of one inch over a one-week period.

Primary students use concrete, pictorial, and verbal representations to describe their algebraic thinking, which lays the foundation necessary for their understanding of how symbols are used to represent more precise algebraic reasoning. The symbol for *equals* (=) is commonly used in primary classrooms, but as mentioned earlier, many young students do not completely understand its meaning. Children typically describe the meaning of the "=" symbol as *the answer is next,* which is a misconception we want to avoid. We can help students understand that the equals symbol

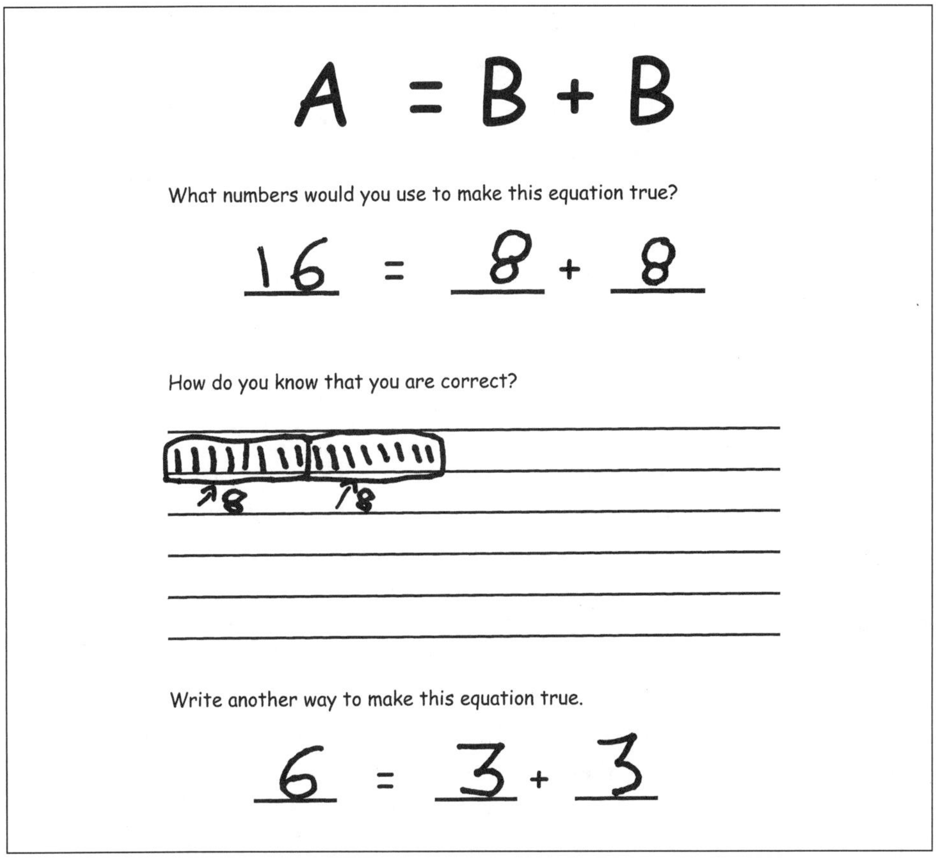

Figure 7–4 *This student was reasoning about algebraic symbols.*

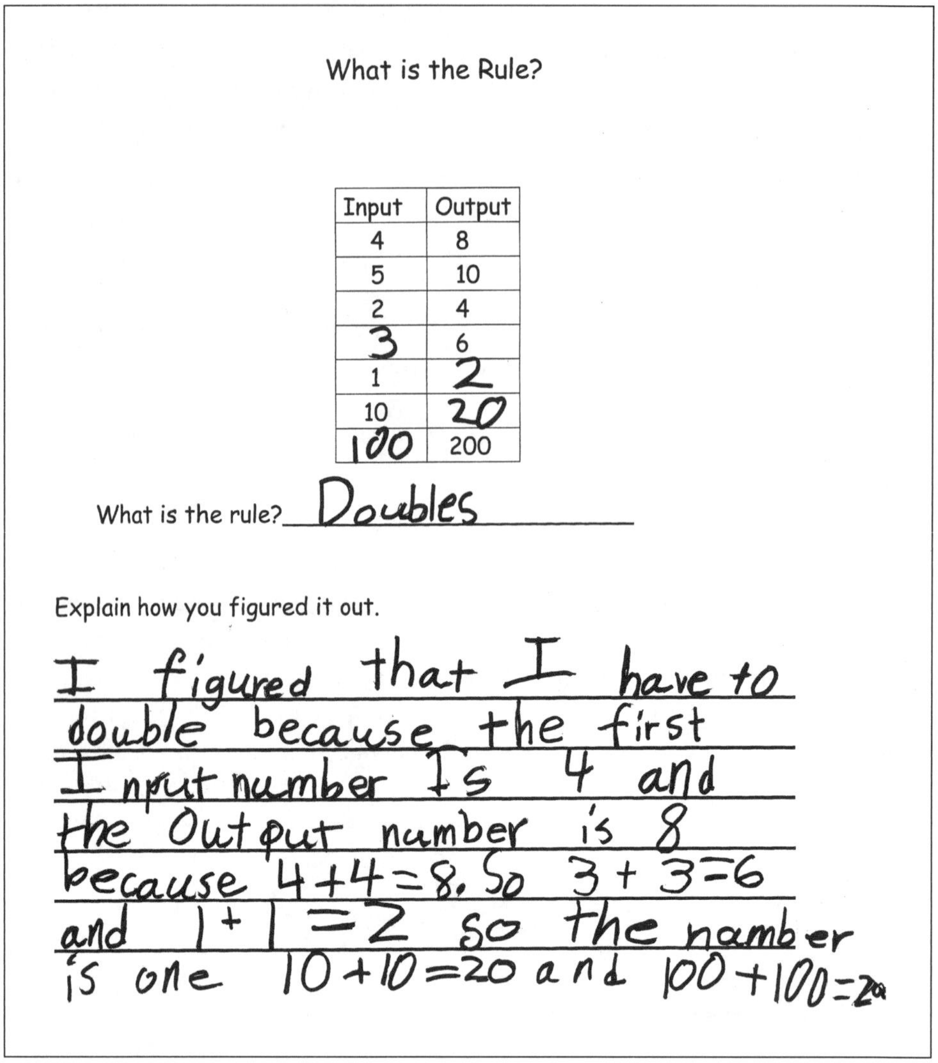

What is the Rule?

Input	Output
4	8
5	10
2	4
3	6
1	2
10	20
100	200

What is the rule? _Doubles_

Explain how you figured it out.

I figured that I have to double because the first Input number Is 4 and the Output number is 8 because 4+4=8. So 3+3=6 and 1+1=2 so the number is one 10+10=20 and 100+100=200

Figure 7–5 *A student explained how he figured out the rule for a function machine activity from the CD.*

means *is the same as* by presenting students with equations in which the *equals* symbol is placed in non-typical ways such as 5 = 2 + 3 or 8 = 8. Students who have been taught traditionally might see these number sentences as incorrect. But asking if equations such as those just suggested are true will generate important algebraic thinking and reasoning from our students and help them develop a deeper understanding of equality.

Primary students are also beginning to form generalizations about number properties. The student dialogues in Chapters 3 and 4 demonstrate how young children do this. It is not necessary for them to know the name or the formal definitions of the properties; rather, they are exploring the properties in concrete experiences. In grades 1 and 2, they are able to state informal conjectures about these properties.

Lesson: Numeral Tiles

The following discussion occurred in a first-grade classroom. Students were using numeral tiles to explore possible placements that could make each number sentence true.

TEACHER: We have some number sentences on the board, and you have the same number sentences on your paper. What do you notice about the number sentences?

STUDENT: One is addition. (___ + ___ = 5)

STUDENT: There's a greater than or less than number sentence. (___< 3)

STUDENT: Don't forget the subtraction one. (___ – ___ = 1)

TEACHER: Use numeral tiles to help you complete the number sentences so they are true. We will only use the numerals 1 through 5, and you can only use each numeral tile once. *(Students are given five minutes to perform the task. The numeral tiles allow students to freely move the numbers in and out of the boxes to explore possible solutions for the number sentences.)*

TEACHER: What did you find out?

STUDENT: I did 2 – 1 = 1.

TEACHER: Would you write the numerals in the boxes on the board to show your work? Remember each numeral can only be used once. *(Student records his work.)*

STUDENT: Can I do 4 + 1 = 5?

STUDENT: We used 1 already!

TEACHER: Hmmmm, what should we do? We used 1 in the subtraction number sentence, and there are no other 1's.

STUDENT: We can use different numerals to make 5.

TEACHER: Explain what you mean.

STUDENT: How about 2 + 3?

STUDENT: 3 works, but we used 2 already.

TEACHER: What are we going to do?

STUDENT: Maybe we could change the subtraction number sentence.

TEACHER: That's an interesting idea. Are there other numbers you can subtract that will give you 1 for an answer?

CLASS: Yes!

TEACHER: Let's record 2 – 1 = 1 under the subtraction number sentence and try a different idea.

STUDENT: I used 5 – 4 = 1.

TEACHER: What do the rest of you think? *(Students are in agreement.)*

TEACHER: *(Student)*, record 5 and 4 in the subtraction boxes. Think about the addition number sentence next. What two numeral tiles can we use to make it a correct number sentence?

STUDENT: Definitely 4 + 1 = 5.

STUDENT: But 4 was just used in the subtraction one.

TEACHER: What else could work?

STUDENT: We used 5 and 4, so we can use 2 and 3. It still makes 5.

STUDENT: I used 2 and 3, too.

TEACHER: Please write it on the board in the addition boxes. Could we say 3 and 2 and still get an answer of 5?

STUDENT: Definitely.

TEACHER: Why is that so?

STUDENT: Because it doesn't matter which way the numbers go. Both ways make 5.

TEACHER: All right. Can we do that in subtraction, too?

STUDENT: No, that would be hard.

TEACHER: Why is that?

STUDENT: Well, if we turn 5 and 4 around, it's 4 – 5, so what do you do with that?

TEACHER: I see. It doesn't matter how the numbers are added, but it does matter with subtraction. *(Students agree.)*

STUDENT: We have one number sentence left.

TEACHER: What does this symbol mean? *(Teacher points to the "<" symbol in the middle number sentence.)*

STUDENT: It's the *less than* sign.

TEACHER: *(To another student), (student)* says this is the *less than* symbol. What does that mean?

STUDENT: The number that comes before it has to be smaller than the number that comes after it. We didn't use 1 yet. And 1 is less than 3. So it works there.

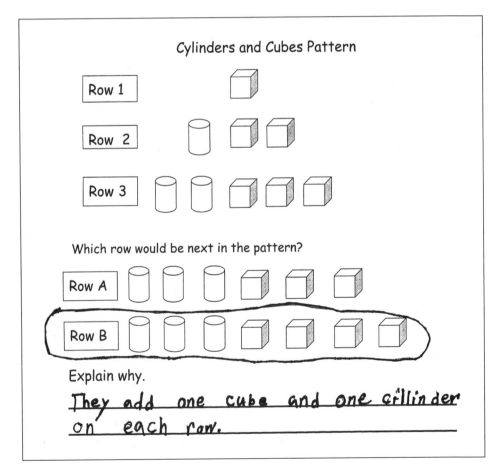

Figure 7–6 *A grade 1 student explained a growing pattern.*

During this lesson, students were investigating and completing equations in several ways, exploring the commutative property of addition, and reasoning about equality. In a brief discussion of the placement of 2 and 3 in the addition number sentence, students demonstrated an understanding of the commutative property of addition. The numeral tiles were used as *variables*, helping students explore the idea that a variable was a symbol that could stand for any one of the numerals 1 through 5. Using the numeral tiles in this manner for specific unknowns is probably the most common way primary students will use variables.

Geometry

The reasoning skills that students are developing in prekindergarten through grade 2 serve an important purpose in the learning of geometry. These reasoning skills support students in exploring and thinking about geometric situations that will enable them to reason about more complex ideas in the intermediate grades and beyond. We must encourage students to describe shapes and their attributes, so it is critical that we provide our students access to geometric manipulatives. Hands-on experiences help students to better notice the common attributes of a class of shapes, such as quadrilaterals. This class of shapes has four sides, but the various shapes that are quadrilaterals—trapezoid, rectangle, square, rhombus, and parallelogram—at first appear different. The following lesson illustrates this important generalization.

Lesson: Sorting Quadrilaterals

Students in a kindergarten classroom were exploring a variety of shapes: quadrilaterals, triangles, pentagons, hexagons, ovals, and circles. These shapes were also different sizes: large and small. After students were given ample time to explore the shapes, they were encouraged to share what they noticed about the shapes.

TEACHER: Tell me something about one of the shapes.
STUDENT: This shape is a circle.
TEACHER: How do you know it's a circle?
STUDENT: It's round.
TEACHER: Does anyone have a shape that is like *(student's)* shape?
STUDENT: I have a little circle.
STUDENT: My circle is squished down.
STUDENT: Oh, that's an oval.
TEACHER: Yes, I see you have an oval. How is an oval like a circle?
STUDENT: They both are curvy.
TEACHER: Who has a shape that is not like an oval or a circle?
STUDENT: I have a triangle.
TEACHER: How is a triangle different from an oval or circle?
STUDENT: The sides are long.
TEACHER: What do you mean the sides are long?

STUDENT: A triangle doesn't turn like the circle because it has straight sides.

TEACHER: Who can tell me something else about a triangle?

STUDENT: It has three sides!

TEACHER: Are there other triangles in your group of shapes?

STUDENT: This triangle is little.

STUDENT: I have a long triangle.

STUDENT: This triangle is pointy.

TEACHER: How many pointy corners are on a triangle?

STUDENT: Three like the sides.

TEACHER: I see different kinds of triangles in this group. Do they all have three sides and three corners? *(Students agree.)* So it doesn't matter if they're different sizes and kinds of triangles?

STUDENT: Well, I have a long triangle, and it has three sides. And *(student's)* triangle is a pretty triangle. It has three sides.

TEACHER: How did you decide to call it a pretty triangle?

STUDENT: I call it that because the sides are the same. It's pretty!

TEACHER: Who can say something about this shape? *(Teacher holds up a square.)*

STUDENT: It's a square. I have one that is tinier than yours.

STUDENT: A square has four sides and four corners.

TEACHER: Are there other shapes with four sides?

STUDENT: Here's one *(the thin rectangle)*. It's skinny.

TEACHER: How many sides does it have?

STUDENT: Four like the square.

TEACHER: So, is it a square?

STUDENT: No, a square is the same.

TEACHER: You mean the same as this? *(Teacher points to the shape pointed out by the student—the thin rectangle.)*

STUDENT: No, the same sides. Squares have all the same sides. That shape has different sides. That one is a skinny rectangle.

TEACHER: I'd like to hear more about the rectangle.

STUDENT: It's long and short on the other sides. Two sides are long and two are short.

TEACHER: Let's explore all the shapes with four sides. Talk with someone near you about another shape that has four sides. *(Teacher walks around and listens to the students' conversations as they talk about the shapes in front of them.)*

TEACHER: Are there any shapes with more than four sides? *(Students talk briefly about the pentagons and the hexagons.)*

The time allowed for students to talk about the shapes they would eventually sort was invaluable. Students were describing attributes that would help them form generalizations among classes of shapes. For example, when students described a variety of triangles (scalene, equilateral, and isosceles), many of the students decided that all of these triangles did indeed have three sides as well as three corners even though some of the triangles looked funny to them. The teacher also connected students' informal language to more precise mathematics vocabulary as they shared descriptions of the different shapes. The teacher next introduced a sorting activity:

TEACHER: I've placed a hoop on the floor to sort our shapes with a special sorting rule. See if you can figure out the rule. You will each choose a shape to put inside the hoop. *(A student places a circle inside the hoop.)*

TEACHER: That shape does not follow the special rule. You can put it outside the hoop.

STUDENT: I want a square in the hoop.

TEACHER: That shape follows the rule. It can stay inside the hoop.

STUDENT: Here's a triangle.

TEACHER: That shape does not follow the rule. *(Student places triangle outside hoop.)* We have a circle and a triangle outside the hoop. I wonder what shapes belong inside the hoop? Think about what shapes could belong inside the hoop.

STUDENT: I have a different triangle. I think it goes outside.

TEACHER: Yes, that triangle goes outside the hoop. What could go inside the hoop?

STUDENT: I think a little square goes inside.

TEACHER: How do you know?

STUDENT: Because there's a square in it, and that's a square, too. Just a little square.

STUDENT: *(very excited)* I have a shape that can go inside. *(Student shows a small rectangle.)*

TEACHER: Yes, that shape can stay inside the hoop. How did you decide to put it inside the hoop?

STUDENT: I looked at the sides of the squares in the hoop. They both had four sides but they were kinda different. This rectangle has four sides, and it's kinda different too. I didn't know if it would work though.

TEACHER: Here's another shape that follows the rule. *(Teacher places a trapezoid inside the hoop.)* This shape goes inside the hoop. What other shapes could go inside?

STUDENT: What about this shape? It has four sides but it looks real different. *(Student holds up a parallelogram.)*

TEACHER: It does fit the rule. Tell us more about the shape you chose.

STUDENT: It has slanted sides. It looks like someone sat on it! They have four lines like the square.

TEACHER: What about this shape? *(Teacher holds up a hexagon.)*

STUDENT: That has to be outside because it has six sides.

TEACHER: What do you notice about the shapes inside the hoop?

STUDENT: Only shapes with four sides go inside.

TEACHER: So, I hear you saying that all of the shapes with four sides go inside the hoop and the other shapes go outside. That is the special rule!

Students had time to sort additional shapes using this rule. They were reasoning deductively as they determined which shapes belonged inside the hoop. (See Figure 7–7.) In order to do this, they needed to identify common attributes of the shapes being sorted. The teacher's goal for the lesson was not for students to learn the names of shapes; rather, it was for them to notice the common attributes that all quadrilaterals share: four sides and four corners. This is an important generalization for young children to understand about geometric plane figures. Another important aspect of the lesson was that students were describing geometric figures. Many of

Figure 7–7 *Students sorted additional shapes during the lesson.*

these descriptions were informal, but the teacher was helping students connect their informal language to more mathematical language. In addition, students were exploring shapes in a variety of sizes, types, and orientations.

In order for our students to reason thoughtfully about geometric concepts, we must provide instruction that involves more than shape definitions. Students benefit from manipulating shapes, drawing and representing shapes in a variety of ways, and exploring spatial concepts. As they compose and decompose plane and solid figures (e.g., placing two triangles together to form a square), they are building an understanding of part-part-whole relationships. The "Sorting Quadrilaterals Lesson" was an example of how to encourage students to first describe and compare shapes before sorting them.

Computer programs are effective learning tools for students to use in the early childhood years. These programs allow children to manipulate shapes in more flexible ways, and their work can be saved and later retrieved. In addition, young students benefit from walking or tracing around shapes, which familiarizes them with the components of shapes. Of course, expect students to describe shapes as they walk or trace around them.

Very young children begin by recognizing a shape by its appearance as a whole. They may only identify a triangle if it is an equilateral triangle, which is how a triangle is typically shown in textbooks, literature, or posters. They will likely say a triangle that is shown as a scalene or isosceles triangle is not a triangle. We can help students to avoid overgeneralizing traditionally shown shapes by giving them access to two-dimensional shapes that are a variety of sizes and types, and positioned in different orientations, as was demonstrated in the lesson on sorting quadrilaterals. It is critical to also expose our students to nonexamples as well. From experiences such as this in prekindergarten and kindergarten, students in grades 1 and 2 will begin to understand how to formulate generalizations among classes of shapes.

Students' work with three-dimensional figures is also crucial for developing geometric concepts. Just as with two-dimensional shapes, it is important to provide students with a variety of solids that are typical and those that are not typical. Giving students sufficient time to explore and manipulate these shapes and then describe them is critical. Prekindergarten and kindergarten students benefit from working with familiar three-dimensional shapes from their environment such as cereal boxes, balls, or soup cans. This helps them to become aware of a wide variety of shapes, and they can begin to describe and reason about the characteristics of these shapes more carefully.

In addition to exposing students to a variety of two- and three-dimensional shapes, we must provide them with experiences that involve thinking spatially. Students' development of visualization and spatial reasoning is strengthened by experiences in which they view shapes from different perspectives. Visualizing in this manner enables students to understand the relationships between two-dimensional and three-dimensional figures. In traditional textbooks, visualization and spatial reasoning are generally not given a strong emphasis as a topic of mathematics. NCTM recommends that students be provided with many experiences in which they are able to visualize and reason to develop their spatial sense. "Spatial sense can be defined as an intuition about shapes and the relationships among shapes. Individuals with spatial sense have a feel for the geometric aspects of their surroundings and the shapes formed by objects in the environment" (Van de Walle and Lovin 2006, 205).

In prekindergarten and kindergarten, students' development of spatial relationships begins with understandings about direction, distance, and location. They describe where objects are in relationship to themselves, which helps them to make sense of their environment. In grades 1 and 2, students build on these understandings and explore ideas of transformations such as flips, slides, and turns. Paper folding and exploring with puzzle pieces, pattern blocks, and tangrams support this understanding in a concrete way. Students' experiences with transformational geometry allow them to identify shapes that are congruent. Their knowledge of location, direction, distance, and transformations will eventually help them move shapes on grids with ordered pairs to represent coordinates that describe points or paths or determine distances.

Primary students are exploring ideas about symmetry. Students build this understanding when they work with examples and nonexamples of symmetry, participate in paper-folding activities, and explore with mirrors, all of which develop their thinking and reasoning about symmetrical relationships.

Developing spatial sense is similar to developing number sense. When students are provided multiple experiences with shapes and spatial relationships over time, their spatial sense is strengthened. These experiences create opportunities for students to reason spatially about shapes and relationships among shapes. Students' thinking and explanations about their spatial reasoning deepen their understanding of geometric concepts and is important in their development as mathematical thinkers.

Here are examples of questions and prompts that promote students' reasoning about geometry and spatial sense:

■ How is your block like *(student's)*? How is it different?

■ If we cut this rectangle, what new shapes do you think we could make?

■ How many different ways can you make a hexagon with the other pattern blocks?

■ If I turn this shape *(a square)*, will it still be the same? Explain why you think so.

■ If I flip this shape, what will it look like?

■ Here are three solid shapes. Can they be stacked? Why do you think so?

■ Describe how to draw this shape.

Lesson: One-Difference Worm

Students in this first-grade classroom were exploring attributes of geometric shapes by using attribute blocks. Attribute blocks include five types of shapes: circles, triangles, rectangles, squares, and hexagons. Each shape has several attributes that vary in the following ways:

■ color: yellow, blue, and red

■ size: small and large

■ thickness: thin and thick

Following is the student dialogue:

TEACHER: We're going to make a one-difference worm with the attribute blocks. Choose three attribute blocks and place them in front of you. Now I'm going to choose the first block that will start the worm. *(Teacher chooses a large, yellow triangle that is also thin.)* What do you notice about the shape?

STUDENT: It's a large yellow triangle.

STUDENT: It's really thin.

TEACHER: You're both right. We said the blocks had different colors, shapes, sizes, and thicknesses. Now look at the blocks you chose and see if you have a block that is different from this block in only one way.

STUDENT: I have one.

TEACHER: Explain why you think your block is different in only one way.

STUDENT: My block is blue.

TEACHER: So they're different by color. Who can tell us how the two blocks are alike?

STUDENT: Both blocks are big.

STUDENT: They're both triangles.

TEACHER: How about their thicknesses?

STUDENT: It works. Both triangles are thin, too.

TEACHER: Your block is different only in color. Place it next to this block so we can begin a one-difference worm. What block could go next to the blue triangle that is also large and thin?

STUDENT: I think it's this one.

TEACHER: Why do you think so?

STUDENT: This one is red, but it's a triangle. It's thin and has three angles. Oh, and it's a large block.

TEACHER: Why does *(student)* think her block goes next?

STUDENT: It's the same except for the color.

TEACHER: Now we have a red triangle that is large and thin. What could go next? *(A student holds up a circular block.)* How is your block different from *(student's)*?

STUDENT: My block doesn't have angles. It's a circle.

TEACHER: What does everyone think? Is *(student's)* block only different by shape?

STUDENT: Well, they're both red and large. And thin!

TEACHER: Your block works. Place it next so we can continue our worm. Who has another block that is different in only one way? *(Another student holds up a circular block.)*

STUDENT: This block works. It's a different color, but it's still a circle.

STUDENT: His block is large, too.

STUDENT: *(Student's)* looks thicker.

TEACHER: I hear you saying that this block is different in color and in thickness. Can we still place it here?

STUDENT: I guess not because my block is different in two ways.

The teacher decided to give students exploration time to locate a shape that might go next in the one-difference worm. Many students began searching through the circular blocks and placing them in different groups by color, size, and thickness.

TEACHER: I noticed that some of you were looking at circles. Hold up your large circles. If your large circle is thick, put it down. *(This leaves a few students holding a thin circle.)* How are your blocks different from the last block in the worm?

STUDENTS: They're different colors.

TEACHER: Yes. There's a blue circle that is thin and large. I also see a yellow circle that is thin and large. Both are different from *(student's)* in only one way. Let's have *(student)* put his shape down first.

STUDENT: I can put my block down next.

TEACHER: How do you know?

STUDENT: Because mine is just a different color.

The manipulatives used in this lesson were helping students think logically about the attributes of the shapes in order to determine an appropriate shape to follow the one-difference rule. This reasoning about geometric relationships helped students think deductively to identify the common attributes between the last block in the "One-Difference Worm" and the new one to be added. Their ability to analyze how shapes were alike or different enabled them to eliminate certain blocks because they were different in more than one way. In the process, students were making informal generalizations about the various shapes. Another important benefit of this activity for students is that it allowed them to hear and use mathematical language in the descriptions and justifications for why certain shapes were different in one way.

Students' work in geometry should involve doing—that is, they should handle a variety of manipulatives and objects to support their understandings of geometric ideas and relationships. "As students sort, build, draw, model, trace, measure, and construct, their capacity to visualize geometric relationships will develop" (NCTM 2000, 165). These experiences strengthen spatial reasoning skills and promote students' abilities to make mathematical arguments to justify conjectures about geometric relationships.

Measurement

Students in prekindergarten through grade 2 are noticing that measurement is constantly present throughout their everyday lives. Not only is measurement intertwined throughout the content standards, it is also integrated in other disciplines such as social studies and science. An important idea for students to understand before they begin grade 3 is that measures are at best approximations, and that we approximate measures daily. Understanding that approximations are acceptable and useful will help students when they are not able to use direct comparison to complete a measurement task.

To lay a firm foundation for measurement, teachers can involve primary students in experiences that involve comparing and ordering objects by measurable attributes. These activities should become a core focus in the primary years. Following is a lesson in which prekindergarten students were engaged in such an experience.

Lesson: Comparing Flowers

During small-group work students were shown three flowers that were different in several ways: heights and width of stems, leaves, and petals. (See Figure 7–8.) The teacher gave a construction-paper flower to each student to describe.*

---

*This lesson was adapted from the work of Carole E. Greenes, Linda Dacey, Mary Cavanagh, Carol R. Findell, Linda Jensen Sheffield, and Marian Small in *Navigating through Problem Solving and Reasoning in Prekindergarten-Kindergarten* (2003, 20–22).

Figure 7–8 *Flowers of different heights and width were presented to prekindergarten students to describe and later order according to clues.*

TEACHER: Here are some flowers. Talk with each other about your flowers. *(Students compared their flowers as they talked together for two minutes.)*

TEACHER: Tell us something about your flower.

STUDENT: It is big.

TEACHER: How do you know it is a big flower?

STUDENT: *(Student)* has a flower littler than mine.

TEACHER: Show us how you know that. *(Student places his flower next to the other student's.)*

STUDENT: If you put them next to each other you can see my flower is bigger.

TEACHER: Oh, you mean like this? *(Teacher places the smaller flower next to student's larger flower but higher to make the tops of both flowers level.)*

STUDENT: *(giggles)* Oh, it looks the same, but the bottoms are not.

STUDENT: No, the bottom has to be the same.

TEACHER: What do you mean?

STUDENT: You have to put them together at the bottom, and then you see my flower is bigger.

TEACHER: I see. This flower is taller than this one *(teacher points to each flower in turn as student speaks)*.

STUDENT: And that flower is smaller.

TEACHER: You are right. That flower is shorter.

TEACHER: *(Student)*, tell us about your flower. *(She has a tall one with a narrow stem.)*

STUDENT: It's like *(student's)* only skinny.

TEACHER: How do you know the flower is skinny?

STUDENT: This part *(pointing to the stem)* is not like the fat part on that flower.

TEACHER: So, the stem on your flower is narrow, and the stem on *(student's)* is wide.

STUDENT: I have a wide stem, too, but it's not tall.

TEACHER: Show us what you mean.

STUDENT: Here it is wide like that one but it is little.

TEACHER: Oh, your flower is short with a wide stem. Tell us about the petals on your flower.

STUDENT: The petals are wide, too.

TEACHER: Hold up your flower if I say something about it.

TEACHER: This flower has a green stem. *(All students hold up their flowers.)* Everyone is holding up a flower. You are really listening! *(Students place flowers on table.)* Hold up your flower if your flower is tall. *(Two students hold up flowers.)*

TEACHER: *(Student)*, how did you know to keep your flower on the table?

STUDENT: My flower is not tall. It's short. *(See Figure 7–9.)*

TEACHER: OK, hold up your flower if it has wide petals. *(Two students hold up their flowers.)* Hold up your flower if it is short and has wide petals.

STUDENT: Mine is both!

TEACHER: What do you mean when you say it is both?

STUDENT: My flower is short and the petals here are fat . . . I mean wide.

TEACHER: We have worked very hard describing our flowers. Let's put them in order on the table. One flower will be first, another one will be next, and then a flower will go last. Here are the clues: The first flower is the tallest flower. *(Students place the flowers side by side to compare and place the tallest flower first.)* Why do you think this flower is the tallest?

STUDENT: It goes higher than any of them. *(Students agree.)*

TEACHER: Here's another clue: The next flower has petals that are wide. *(Students compare the remaining two flowers.)* Tell me how you are deciding which flower to place after the tallest flower.

STUDENT: Well, see this flower has skinny petals, but this one has fat ones that are wide. A bug would like that one!

TEACHER: What flower is last?

STUDENT: This one! It's the only one left. It has to go last. It's real small.

These young learners were engaged in mathematics that will lay the groundwork for understanding important ideas about measurement and also help them to reason about mathematical relationships. As students were describing the flowers, they were using comparative words such as *tall, wide,* and *narrow.* They ordered the flowers based on clues, which helped them to reason deductively. The teacher encouraged them to test their conjectures about which flower the clue was referring to by expecting them to explain their thinking. Students were also ordering objects by height and width, recognizing attributes of shapes, and using ordinal terms in this simple yet fun activity.

Primary students' instruction in measurement focuses on length; however, other areas of measurement such as weight, time, area, volume, and temperature should be explored by students. Children develop understandings about measurement concepts in the following ways:

Figure 7–9 *A prekindergarten student described her flower.*

- recognizing that objects have measurable attributes and describing these attributes;

- comparing objects by matching (longer, shorter, wider, taller);

- comparing objects with nonstandard units;

- comparing objects with standard units;

- choosing efficient tools and units for specific measurements, and;

- creating and using formulas to count units that identify measurements.

Students' measurement work in prekindergarten through grade 2 focuses mainly on the first three understandings listed above. These experiences support them in the intermediate grades when they compare objects using standard units and choose units that measure specific objects more efficiently. All of these experiences are foundational for their understanding of the abstract formulas they will encounter in higher grades.

Measurement naturally connects geometry and number. This is evident in students' everyday lives. For example, they reason about which types of blocks will produce the highest tower, how much paper must be cut to wrap a box, or whether they have enough money to buy a snack. The discussions we have with our students as they explain their thinking about the various measurement concepts they are learning will help them develop the mathematical language associated with measurement. Of course, the use of measurement vocabulary in context is critical.

Young children's early ideas of weight are developed when they consider which object is heavier or lighter. Balances allow them to see concretely the effect of an object's weight; that is, a heavier object will force a balance to go down on one side. The later use of a scale attaches a numerical value to a weight. Children's explorations of capacity and volume are done informally, and they are not yet placing a numerical value on these attributes of measurements. We can promote reasoning about capacity and volume by asking students to explain how they know, for example, which container of several will hold more water or cubes.

Time concepts are complex ideas for young children. Prekindergarten and kindergarten students begin learning about time through their daily routines. They are learning specific words such as *morning* and *afternoon* as well as relational words such as *tomorrow, now*, and *sometimes* to describe when events happen. In grades 1 and 2, students' work with duration words such as *seconds, minutes, hours, date, days, months, seasons,* and *years* further develop their understandings about time. To help students better understand the duration of time, we must be careful when setting time limits on tasks. For example, when we say, "just a minute," we must be sure it truly is a minute; otherwise, students may develop incorrect ideas about the duration of a minute. Calendar routines are often implemented in the primary years to help children understand many ideas about duration. The student discussions we facilitate about the calendar activities our students complete promote their reasoning about time.

We stated earlier the importance of students recognizing the value of approximations in a variety of measurement situations. These experiences support students in determining whether measurements are reasonable. The language of estimation begins early as children informally use words such as *close to, almost, way over,* or *a little smaller* in the context of their estimations. In grades 1 and 2, students' estimates involve numerical values such as estimating how many cubes will be necessary to measure the length of a desk. They develop personal benchmarks that help approximate their measurements such as using the width of two fingers as a substitute for about one inch. Expect students to explain how they make their estimates and to check their thinking by actually measuring the object. Discussion of the reasonableness of estimates is important in developing students' estimation skills.

CLASSROOM-TESTED TIP

Here are questions and prompts that you can use to promote students' reasoning about measurement concepts:

- Which is longer (shorter)? How do you know?

- Which shape will take the most color tiles to cover it? Why do you think so?

■ To cover this same shape, would it take more beans or more color tiles? Why?

■ How many times can you write your first name in one minute? How many times can you write your whole name in one minute? How did you decide?

■ Which object is lighter? How did you decide?

■ Explain why your estimate for the length of the book makes sense to you.

Concepts about area are more complex for young learners because they have to think about more than one dimension. However, they are beginning to understand the conceptual difference of how long an object is and how much space a drawing may cover.

Lesson: Estimating Area

The following dialogue from a second-grade classroom* demonstrates how students were reasoning about the possible area of three similar shapes:

TEACHER: What do you notice about the three rectangles on your paper? *(Students share a few observations about the rectangles, which are similar in size.)* If you use one-inch color tiles, which rectangle would need the most tiles to cover it? Place one color tile inside each shape to help you think about this. *(Students are given about 15 seconds.)* Now talk with someone about what you think. *(Students are given 30 seconds.)* Write an estimate for how many color tiles you think will be needed to cover each rectangle. *(Students record an estimate near the letter identifying each rectangle.)*.

TEACHER: How did you decide on an estimate for Rectangle A?

STUDENT: I counted squares I made up in my head, and that's how I got 20.

TEACHER: How did you think about that?

STUDENT: One tile took up half of the space going across. I did two's about ten times.

STUDENT: I saw how big the rectangle was, and I tried to make my fingers as big as a color tile. I kept putting them down and counted 16.

STUDENT: I used two of my fingers and kept moving them, too, but I think it's 14 tiles.

STUDENT: I just guessed and got 19.

TEACHER: What is your estimate for the number of tiles it will take to cover Rectangle B? *(Students state estimates, which are mostly fewer than those for Rectangle A. Each time they are expected to state how they decided on an estimate.)*

---

*This lesson was adapted from *The Super Source—Color Tiles, Grades K-2* (1996, 86–89). Vernon Hills, IL: ETA/Cuisenaire.

TEACHER: *(Student)*, I see you estimated Rectangle B will take 19 tiles, and you estimated Rectangle A will take 14 tiles. Why do you think so?

STUDENT: Rectangle B is wider than the other one. It looks like it'll hold more. It was kinda hard to decide because B is wider, but it's shorter than A.

TEACHER: I also noticed that many of you think Rectangle B will take fewer tiles to cover than Rectangle A. How did you decide?

STUDENT: I disagree with *(student)*. I think Rectangle B is smaller than A because it is not as long. If you cut it apart, it looks like you could put it inside Rectangle A with a little space left over.

STUDENT: I used my fingers like I did for Rectangle A and got less squares.

TEACHER: What about Rectangle C?

STUDENT: It takes up more space than Rectangle B, and it's way wider.

TEACHER: Compare the sizes of Rectangle A and Rectangle C. Are they similar or very different?

STUDENT: I think if we cut Rectangle A apart and put the pieces on top of Rectangle C, they would fit together pretty good.

TEACHER: I see your estimates for Rectangle A and C are really close. Were you thinking the same as *(student)*?

STUDENT: I did like *(student)*. Only I thought C would stick out some when on top of A.

STUDENT: I used the tops of my two fingers on both rectangles, and that's how I got my estimates so close.

STUDENT: Rectangles A and C look like they go together. B looks smaller than them.

TEACHER: Check your estimates with the color tiles. When you finish covering a rectangle, record how many tiles it took to cover it beside your original estimate. *(Students work for about 10 minutes. See Figure 7–10.)*

TEACHER: What did you find out?

STUDENT: On Rectangle B, I estimated 13 and it took 12. That's close! Pretending I had color tiles really helped me.

TEACHER: Let's think about that. Some of you said Rectangle A and C seemed close in size. Was your actual count for C close to the actual count for A? *(Many students agree.)*

STUDENT: C was tricky. It's shorter than A, but it's wider. And it needed the most tiles to cover it!

In this activity, students were thinking and reasoning about mathematics that included concepts about measurement, number, and geometry. Students were exploring the relationship between shape and area in order to compare and determine the area of the three similar shapes. The teacher encouraged students to first estimate how many color tiles would be needed to cover each shape, and then she expected them to explain how their estimates were formed. This is important for students to do because they will be reasoning about their process of estimating. And other students benefit from hearing classmates' strategies for thinking about estimation. One student simply guessed Rectangle A's area, but was later observed exploring with an estimation strategy described earlier by a classmate.

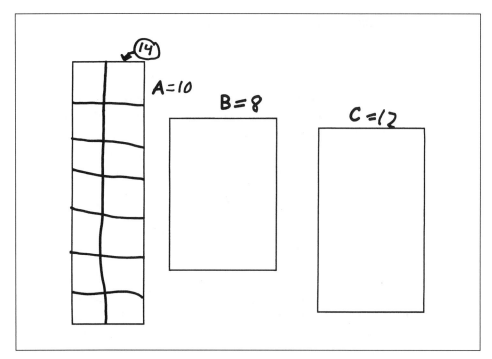

Figure 7–10 *This shows a student's partial work as she informally estimated the area of three similar shapes.*

The teacher's choice of the word *cover* helped students to develop an initial understanding of area as a *measure of covering*. This understanding will support students in later years as they make sense of the formulas traditionally used for finding area. In addition, working with similar rectangles prompted students to apply reasoning when thinking about the possible number of color tiles needed to cover each of them.

Data Analysis and Probability

Prerequisites skills necessary for students' abilities to collect, organize, display, and analyze data are activities that involve sorting and classifying, which also include identification of objects' attributes. These skills are also important in developing foundational understandings in other content standards, particularly algebra. Sorting and classifying skills are utilized in other discipline areas such as literacy, social studies, and science.

Students' curiosity about their immediate environment encourages them to pose questions that focus on information about their peers. Young children begin by collecting data in the form of *real graphs*. These graphs use concrete objects or students themselves to represent the collected data. Yes/no surveys are simple surveys of observable attributes of classmates and are easily conducted by young students. They learn that check marks or tally marks are useful in recording multiple responses in an efficient way when they are collecting data in a survey. Students should become familiar with multiple data displays such as pictographs or bar graphs. They benefit when we expect them to decide on titles and labels for their data displays and to explain why these suggestions are appropriate.

Describing and comparing collected data is critical. When beginning any data discussions, the most important question to ask students is: "What do you notice about today's data?" This question gives students an opportunity to reason about the information in a way that makes sense to them. Allow about three to five minutes for students to share their observations. Teachers state that traditional questions generally are not necessary when asking this open-ended question because students naturally share information about data that focuses on concepts such as *more, less, equal, odd, even, how many more, counting,* etc.

Lesson: Pencils in Our Desks

Students in a first-grade classroom were asked to count the number of pencils inside their desks. Each student's name and count was recorded in a chart, and the number of pencils ranged from one to thirteen. The teacher then facilitated a discussion of how a pictograph could be constructed to reflect the student data collected. Students decided they would call the graph, "Number of Pencils in Our Desks." They proceeded to make decisions about the labels for the graph and how the data should be recorded. They were learning that a pictograph uses a common picture or symbol to represent the data collected.

The following day this discussion occurred:

TEACHER: Yesterday we made a pictograph about the number of pencils in our desks. *(See Figure 7–11.)* We're going to use some of our information from the graph to help us in today's math lesson. I used part of the data to make up a logic problem. Listen to the clues and see if you can figure out the name of the students the clues are describing:

Jose, Ida, Sophi, Camron, Jada, Shannon, and Quincy have pencils in their desks.
  Jose has the fewest pencils.
  Ida and Sophi both have one more pencil than Jose.
  Camron and Jada have double the number of pencils that Ida and Sophi have.
  Shannon has the greatest number of pencils.

TEACHER: Think about the clues. You can use any clue you want to start. What do you think?
STUDENT: Start with Jose. He only has one pencil.
TEACHER: So Jose has one pencil. What do you think we should think about next?
STUDENT: Go to the clue about Ida and Sophi.
TEACHER: Why did you choose that clue next?
STUDENT: Because they have one more pencil than Jose. That's two, and I see places with two X's.
TEACHER: Let's look at the clue about Camron and Jada. It says they have double the number of pencils that Ida and Sophi have. What does *double* mean?

Number of Pencils in Our Desks	
?	X
?	XXXXXX
?	XX
?	XXXXXXXXXXXXX
?	XX
?	XXXX
?	XXXX
Key: **X**=1 pencil	

Figure 7–11 *This pictograph showed the teacher's graph that was made from data collected by students in the previous day's lesson. It became a logical thinking task.*

STUDENT: *Double* means that you have two things.

STUDENT: I'm not sure what you mean.

TEACHER: Could you tell us more about your way of thinking?

STUDENT: I mean if you have two and you add two more. When you double two, you get four.

TEACHER: Thank you for explaining that for us. Who has another example of what *double* means?

STUDENT: You add the same number again. Like one. Double one is two.

TEACHER: Suppose you have three. What is double three?

STUDENT: Six! You add another three to three.

TEACHER: What about double ten?

CLASS: Twenty!

TEACHER: The clue says: Camron and Jada have double the number of pencils that Ida and Sophi have. How many pencils do they each have?

STUDENT: They have four.

TEACHER: How do you know?

STUDENT: Ida and Sophi have two. Double two is four.

TEACHER: The last clue says that Shannon has the greatest number of pencils. Where do you think her name belongs on the graph?

STUDENT: That's easy. She's the thirteen. That's the biggest number of all of them.

TEACHER: What are we going to do about Quincy's name? I didn't see a clue for Quincy.

STUDENT: It's beside the row of six X's.

TEACHER: How do you know?

STUDENT: That's the only one without a name.

Students were reasoning deductively as they solved a logic problem based on real data collected in the previous day's math lesson. Students were challenged to think about several constraints as they thought about the clues and then encouraged to explain their solutions by checking them against each clue. Although students were presented the option of choosing any clue to begin solving the problem, they chose to begin with the first clue. Later, as students' experiences grow, consider placing clues out of order to challenge students. This encourages them to think about all of the clues and to consider which clues are more helpful to use first, an important reasoning strategy. (See Figures 7–12 and 7–13.)

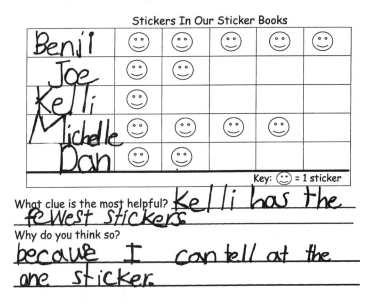

Figure 7–12 *A student explained which clue was the most helpful in solving this reasoning task.*

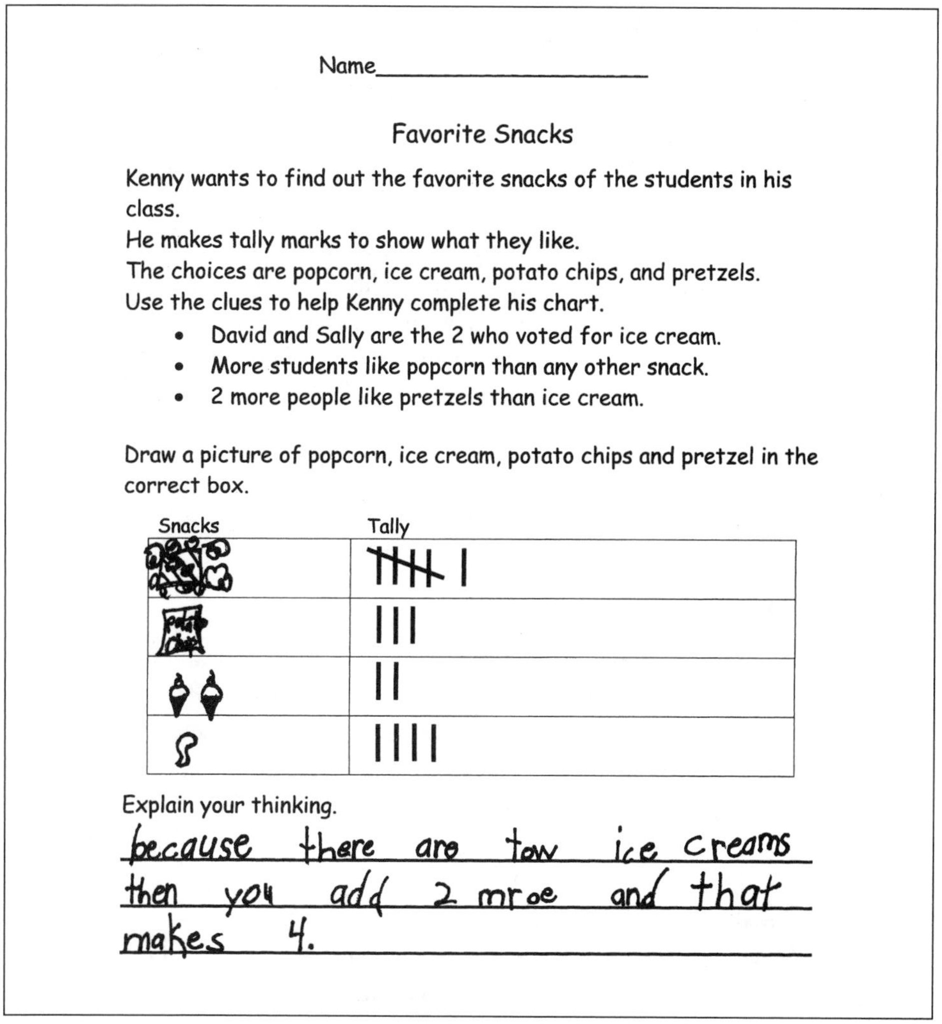

Name_____

Favorite Snacks

Kenny wants to find out the favorite snacks of the students in his class.
He makes tally marks to show what they like.
The choices are popcorn, ice cream, potato chips, and pretzels.
Use the clues to help Kenny complete his chart.
- David and Sally are the 2 who voted for ice cream.
- More students like popcorn than any other snack.
- 2 more people like pretzels than ice cream.

Draw a picture of popcorn, ice cream, potato chips and pretzel in the correct box.

Snacks	Tally
(popcorn drawing)	ᛚᚼᚼ I
(potato chips drawing)	III
(ice cream drawing)	II
(pretzel drawing)	IIII

Explain your thinking.

because there are tow ice creams then you add 2 mroe and that makes 4.

Figure 7–13 *A student reasoned about how he solved this logical thinking task from the CD.*

Probability

The focus for probability in the primary years is on the most basic concepts, and vocabulary such as *impossible* and *certain* can be used to express these ideas. This basic vocabulary of probability must be used in the context of a familiar situation for students. For example, *It is certain we will be eating lunch.* Or *It is impossible that we will stay overnight at school.* Probability is a difficult concept for young children. Some of this difficulty lies in the vocabulary associated with probability. Family members and other adults often use the word *probably* with mixed meanings. When they answer, *probably*, it could mean yes or no depending on the day! We can support our youngest learners by helping them to develop an intuitive understanding of chance that will then become a foundation for more complex ideas in grades 3 through 5.

Lesson: Teddy Bears in a Bag

Students in this kindergarten classroom were considering probability in an informal and exploratory manner. A bag containing five teddy bears—four red and one blue—was shown to them although they could not see inside the bag.

TEACHER: I have a bag with five teddy bears. The colors of the teddy bears are red and blue. See if you can predict how many teddy bears are red and how many teddy bears are blue. You each get a turn to take one teddy bear out of the bag without looking. Then we will put the teddy bear back in the bag. After everyone has taken a turn choosing a bear and placing it back into the bag, we will predict the colors of the teddy bears. How can we remember what color is chosen each time?

STUDENT: We could write the color.

STUDENT: We could do like we do when we keep track of the lunches we want. *(Student points to the day's lunch tally chart.)*

STUDENT: When we get red, we could make a line.

TEACHER: You're right. We could make a tally mark to keep track of each color chosen. *(Two students volunteer to be the recorder: one to record red tally marks and the other to record blue tally marks.)* Remember, we are choosing a teddy bear without looking and then taking a peek once it's outside of the bag. *(The first student reaches in the bag and pulls out a bear.)*

STUDENT: I got a red teddy bear. *(Student shows bear and then drops it back into the bag.)*

STUDENT: I'll make a tally line on my side.

TEACHER: We have one tally mark on the red side of the tally chart. I wonder what will come out next? *(A new student reaches into the bag.)*

STUDENT: I got a red teddy bear, too.

STUDENT: Me next. Hey, I got red, too!

TEACHER: Oh, my! So far we have only chosen red teddy bears.

STUDENT: Look, I got a red again. Yeah, the reds will get more and more.

STUDENT: I got red. Is blue really in the bag?

STUDENT: Yay! I got a blue teddy bear so blue is in the bag!

TEACHER: Look at the tally marks so we can see how many of each color has been chosen so far.

STUDENT: We have more than five bears.

TEACHER: What do you mean?

STUDENT: We picked a lot. I can count the marks on the chart, and there's more than five up there.

TEACHER: When we all get a turn to peek, we will predict how many of the five bears we think are red and how many bears we think are blue.

STUDENT: My turn. I got red again.

STUDENT: I got blue. *(This continues until each student has had a turn to randomly choose a bear, the result has been recorded, and the bear has been placed back into the bag. See Figure 7–14.)*

TEACHER: Look at the tally marks on the chart. What do you think?

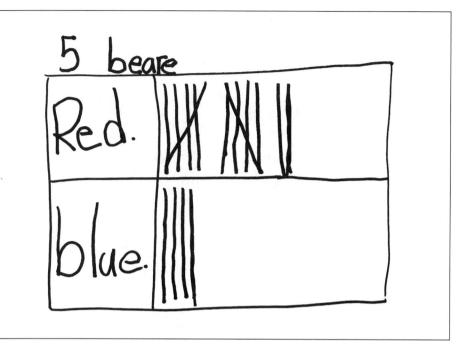

Figure 7–14 *A student recorded the results of students randomly pulling teddy bears from a bag.*

STUDENT: There are a lot of red and just a little blue.

STUDENT: Blue had a very little.

TEACHER: How many students pulled out a red bear?

STUDENT: Twelve.

TEACHER: How many pulled out a blue bear?

STUDENT: Four.

TEACHER: What can someone tell me about the numbers of tallies?

STUDENT: There's a lot more red tallies than blue.

TEACHER: There are only five bears in the bag. When you took a bear out, you put it back into the bag after we saw its color. Do you think there are more blue bears in the bag? Or do you think there are more red bears in the bag? Talk to a friend about what you think. *(Students talk for about 30 seconds.)*

STUDENT: I think there are more red bears.

TEACHER: Why do you think *(student)* thinks there are more red bears in the bag?

STUDENT: Because the red was more on the tallies.

TEACHER: I'd like to know what everybody thinks. Draw five bears. Color how many bears you think are red. Then color the number of bears you think are blue. *(Students work on their predictions for about 15 minutes.)*

TEACHER: *(Student),* I see you made three red bears and two blue bears. *(See Figure 7–15.)* Tell me why you do not have more blue bears.

STUDENT: The blue did not have a lot of tallies so I think there is a little bit.

STUDENT: I made less blue bears because it did not win.

TEACHER: So if the blue had won the tallies what would that mean?

STUDENT: It means that you had more blue bears.

Figure 7–15 *A student's representation of how many bears could be red and how many bears could be blue inside the bag.*

TEACHER: *(Student)*, I see you made four red bears. What will you color this bear?

STUDENT: Blue, because *(student)* picked a blue bear, so I know you have a blue bear in there. Red won so I made it more.

TEACHER: If I wanted blue to win, what would I need in the bag?

STUDENT: You could have all blue teddy bears!

TEACHER: What else?

STUDENT: Or only one red teddy bear.

TEACHER: Are there more ways?

STUDENT: You could have two red bears and three blue bears. That's it, because next it would be more red bears

TEACHER: I see that many of you have more red teddy bears in your pictures. I'm going to show you what is in the bag. *(The bag is emptied to show four red teddy bears and one blue teddy bear.)*

Kindergarten students were informally thinking and reasoning about the possibility of pulling a red or blue teddy bear from the bag. The idea of "peeking" at a teddy bear that was randomly chosen was appealing to them. Because of their immature un-

Frank's Pencils

Frank has ten pencils in his desk. One of his pencils is blue and nine of his pencils are yellow. If Frank closes his eyes and reaches in the desk to get a pencil, what color pencil will he probably get?

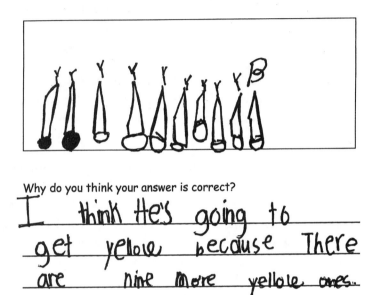

Why do you think your answer is correct?

I think He's going to get yellow because There are nine more yellow ones.

Figure 7–16 *A grade 2 student reasoned about probability in this CD task.*

derstanding of probability, many had difficulty remembering there were only five teddy bears in the bag and needed to be reminded. When students analyzed the color data collected from the numerous "peeks," they reasoned fairly accurately about what the teddy bear colors could be inside the bag. The teacher's expectation that they represent their predictions in a drawing helped them to visualize the possible contents of the bag.

Final Thoughts

The interconnectedness of the mathematics process and content standards is demonstrated throughout this chapter in the student dialogues. When concepts are taught in this manner, students do not view mathematics as an isolated subject that has little relevance to them. Instead they understand that the math they are learning can be applied to other disciplines, to other mathematical ideas, and to real-world situations. They will be internalizing important ideas about mathematics as they engage in problem-solving tasks that promote reasoning and as they communicate and represent their reasoning in different ways. By presenting experiences that encourage our students to reason daily, we are enabling them to see that reasoning is relevant in all areas of their lives.

Questions for Discussion

1. Reasoning takes a variety of forms across the content standards. In geometry, spatial reasoning is often not a topic explored in textbooks. Why is spatial reasoning important, and how does it help students in later grades? Discuss with colleagues several ideas for lessons that will develop students' spatial reasoning.

2. Algebra is frequently referred to as the gatekeeper to higher mathematics learning. How will you encourage your students to think algebraically? Do you see this as something that can be done in all areas of mathematics? Why do you feel this way?

3. Reasoning about important mathematical ideas and relationships helps students make sense of math and relate it to other ideas they will be learning in higher grades. Think about all of the content areas to answer this question: What are a few important ideas you would like your students to reason and make conjectures about? How will formulating generalizations about these ideas and developing mathematical explanations and arguments to justify them support your students in later grades?

If students are consistently expected to explore, question, conjecture, and justify their ideas, they learn that mathematics should make sense, rather than believing that mathematics is a set of arbitrary rules and formulas.

—Robert E. Reys, Mary M. Lindquist, Diana V. Lambdin, Nancy L. Smith, and Marilyn N. Suydam, *Helping Children Learn Mathematics*

Reasoning is viewed as a necessary process for ensuring that students understand mathematical ideas and relationships. It is a way to make the abstract nature of mathematics more understandable. Understandings about mathematics are further enhanced by an instructional program that presents knowledge that is connected and integrated and that helps students to think and reason about new knowledge by connecting their reasoning to what they already know.

Focusing our instruction so that students become efficient problem solvers who reason effectively to make sense of the mathematics they are learning is a challenging goal. We hope this book will assist you in implementing this important change in your instructional program, a change that will greatly benefit your students for the rest of their lives. Students' ability to reason develops over time. The problems you select for your students to solve and the questions you ask of students in your daily discussions will help them learn how to select and use different types of reasoning such as intuitive, inductive, and deductive thinking.

Through the establishment of a positive classroom environment, you are setting the stage for students' productive reasoning to occur. An environment in which students can feel safe and comfortable as they collaboratively share how they are reasoning supports them in making conjectures and developing mathematical arguments.

By providing your students with problems that are engaging, challenging, and authentic with relevant connections, you will enable them to strengthen their reasoning skills and acquire mathematics knowledge through problem solving. These problems will promote rich discussions that will support your students' reasoning abilities.

Through your facilitation of these daily student discussions, you are enabling your students to become thoughtful thinkers as they must first reflect and clarify their thinking before expressing reasoning that is clearly understood. Your students will have multiple opportunities to listen to their classmates' thinking and reasoning, which enhances their own learning. When we make students' views the focus of our discussions, students are encouraged to listen to one another's reasoning and to question each other when reasoning needs clarification. Not only does this support students' reasoning abilities, but it also enables them to have a confident attitude about mathematics.

Through developing a repertoire of carefully chosen questions, you will enable your students to focus on effective reasoning about a variety of mathematical ideas and relationships. Asking questions that cause your students to ponder about mathematical ideas will encourage reasoning and facilitate productive learning. Model for your students that they should also question and reason about what others have shared regarding the mathematics they are learning. You will be helping your students to ask questions of themselves and others, which will allow them to monitor their own learning and become independent and powerful mathematical thinkers.

Through a variety of engaging activities on the CD, your students will develop, extend, and refine their reasoning skills. These activities provide you with evidence of their developing reasoning skills and mathematics knowledge. The many reasoning tools demonstrated in the book, and on the CD, will help your students learn to organize their thinking and reasoning so that they become more independent problem solvers. The convenience you have in modifying the CD activities to appropriately meet your students' needs, interests, and skills will certainly enhance your instruction.

The classroom environment we create to support our students' reasoning skills should be one that is integrated with the remaining process standards of problem solving, communication, representation, and connections. As you plan your instruction each school year, include daily instruction that infuses the process standards to help your students become proficient mathematical thinkers. Allowing your students to make connections among mathematical ideas, to other disciplines, and to their everyday lives will greatly enhance their reasoning abilities.

An important goal we want for all of our students is to ensure that students are provided multiple opportunities to acquire critical reasoning skills that will serve them as they grapple with more complicated mathematics topics in later grades. As you are implementing new expectations into your classroom routine, you will encounter shared reasoning that contains flaws or misconceptions. We must convey to our students that flaws can occur in anyone's reasoning, and that the follow-up investigation to make sense of the misconception is indeed valuable to everyone's learning.

When our students know their thinking and reasoning are valued, and a necessary part of their development as mathematical thinkers, we will have indeed accomplished an important goal. As mathematics educators we want all our students to understand that reasoning is a central part of every mathematics lesson, and that they are responsible for expressing their reasoning and understanding the reasoning of others. This ability to reason allows our students to make sense of the mathematics they are learning, and it enables them to become students who are willing to explore, investigate, and challenge mathematical ideas. Not only will our students benefit in amazing ways if we work with this goal in mind, but we will also.

Additional Resources for Reasoning and Proof

The following resources are meant to support you as you explore the reasoning and proof standard in prekindergarten through grade 2 classrooms. You will find a variety of text resources—books that will provide you with additional reasoning activities or instructional strategies. A list of math websites is included to supply you with classroom tasks, electronic manipulative ideas, or teacher resources. And for additional professional development, several video products are listed that allow you to view mathematical reasoning in primary classrooms and reflect on the video lessons, whether alone or with a group of your colleagues.

Text Resources

The following text resources provide a variety of activities and strategies for supporting students as they develop their reasoning skills.

Burns, Marilyn. 1982. *Math for Smarty Pants*. Boston: Little, Brown.
Cameron, A., M. Dolk, C. Twomey Fosnot, and S. Hersch. 2005. *Young Mathematicians at Work, PreK–3*. Portsmouth, NH: Heinemann.
Cavanagh, Mary, Linda Dacey, Carol R. Findell, Carole E. Greenes, Linda Jensen Sheffield, and Marian Small. 2004. *Navigating through Number and Operations in Prekindergarten—Grade 2*. Reston, VA: National Council of Teachers of Mathematics.
Coates, Grace Davila, and Jean Kerr Stenmark. 1997. *Family Math for Young Children*. Berkeley, CA: Lawrence Hall of Science.
Confer, Chris. 2005. *Teaching Number Sense—K*. Sausalito, CA: Math Solutions Publications.
———. 2005. *Teaching Number Sense—Grade 1*. Sausalito, CA: Math Solutions Publications
Copley, Juanita V. 2000. *The Young Child and Mathematics*. Washington, DC: National Association for the Education of Young Children.
———. ed. 2004. *Showcasing Mathematics for the Young Child: Activities for Three-, Four-, and Five-Year-Olds*. Reston, VA: National Council of Teachers of Mathematics.

Dacey, Linda, Mary Cavanagh, Carol R. Findell, Carole E. Greenes, Linda Jensen Sheffield, and Marian Small. 2003. *Navigating through Measurement in Prekindergarten—Grade 2*. Reston, VA: National Council of Teachers of Mathematics.

Findell, Carol R., Mary Cavanagh, Linda Dacey, Carole E. Greenes, Linda Jensen Sheffield, and Marian Small. 2004. *Navigating through Problem Solving and Reasoning in Grade 1*. Reston, VA: National Council of Teachers of Mathematics.

Findell, Carol R., Marian Small, Mary Cavanagh, Linda Dacey, Carole E. Greenes, and Linda Jenson Sheffield. 2001. *Navigating through Geometry in Prekindergarten—Grade 2*. Reston, VA: National Council of Teachers of Mathematics.

Greenes, Carole, and Carol Findell. 1999. *Groundworks: Algebraic Thinking—Grade 1*. Chicago, IL: Creative Publications.

Greenes, Carole E., Linda Dacey, Mary Cavanagh, Carol R. Findell, Linda Jensen Sheffield, and Marian Small. 2003. *Navigating through Problem Solving and Reasoning in Prekindergarten—Kindergarten*. Reston, VA: National Council of Teachers of Mathematics.

Greenes, Carole, Mary Cavanagh, Linda Dacey, Carol Findell, and Marian Small. 2001. *Navigating through Algebra in Prekindergarten—Grade 2*. Reston, VA: National Council of Teachers of Mathematics.

Hersch, S., A. Cameron, M. Dolk, C. Twomey Fosnot. 2004. *Fostering Children's Mathematical Development, Grades PreK–3*. Portsmouth, NH: Heinemann.

O'Connell, Susan. 2000. *Introduction to Problem Solving: Strategies for the Elementary Math Classroom*. Portsmouth, NH: Heinemann.

———. 2005. *Now I Get It: Strategies for Building Confident and Competent Mathematicians, K–6*. Portsmouth, NH: Heinemann.

Rotz, Leyani von, and Marilyn Burns. 2002. *Lessons for Algebraic Thinking, Grades K–2*. Sausalito, CA: Math Solutions Publications.

Scharton, Susan. 2005. *Teaching Number Sense—Grade 2*. Sausalito, CA: Math Solutions Publications.

Sheffield, Linda Jensen, Mary Cavanagh, Linda Dacey, Carol R. Findell, Carole E. Greenes, and Marian Small. 2002. *Navigating through Data Analysis and Probability in Prekindergarten—Grade 2*. Reston, VA: National Council of Teachers of Mathematics.

Small, Marian, Linda Jensen Sheffield, Mary Cavagagh, Linda Dacey, Carol R. Findell, and Carole E. Geenes. 2004. *Navigating through Problem Solving and Reasoning in Grade 2*. Reston, VA: National Council of Teachers of Mathematics.

The Super Source: Color Tiles, Grades K–2. 1996. Vernon Hills, IL: ETA/Cuisenaire.

Trafton, Paul R. and Diane Thiessen. 1997. *Learning Through Problems: Number Sense and Computational Strategies*. Portsmouth, NH: Heinemann.

Van de Walle, John A., and LouAnn H. Lovin. 2006. *Teaching Student-Centered Mathematics, Grades K–3*. Vol. 1. Boston: Pearson Education.

Westley, Joan. 1994. *Puddle Questions*. Mountain View, CA: Creative.

Web Resources

The following websites provide a variety of lesson ideas, classroom resources, and ready-to-use math reasoning tasks.

www.abcteach.com/directory/basics/math/problem_solving—The problem-solving and reasoning activities on this abcteach website provide opportunities for talking and writing about math.

www.aimsedu.org/index.html—This AIMS (Activities Integrating Mathematics and Science) website includes sample activities, information on AIMS professional development, an online store, and other teacher resources.

www.etacuisenaire.com—This website showcases the products of the ETA/Cuisenaire Company, which is a supplier of classroom mathematics manipulatives and teacher resource materials.

www.heinemann.com—This website of Heinemann Publishing is a source for a variety of professional development resources for teachers.

www.illuminations.nctm.org—Explore a variety of reasoning activities on this website of the National Council of Teachers of Mathematics.

www.learner.org/channel/courses/teachingmath/gradesk_2/session_02/index.html—This Annenberg Media site offers a free, self-paced online course to help teachers better understand the reasoning standard, including lesson excerpts, video clips, and reflection questions.

www.learningresources.com—This website showcases the products of the Learning Resources Company, which supplies a variety of mathematics manipulatives and teacher resource materials.

www.math.com/teachers.html—This site offers lesson plans, classroom resources, links to "free stuff," and online tutorial assistance.

www.nctm.org—On this National Council of Teachers of Mathematics (NCTM) website you will find information on regional and national conferences sponsored by NCTM, as well as a variety of professional development materials.

www.puzzlemaker.com—Create crossword puzzles and word searches for key math vocabulary using this website.

www.wits.ac.za/ssproule/pow.htm—This website lists links to problem-of-the-week sites at all academic levels and includes a site rating system. The problems provide opportunities to get students thinking and reasoning about math ideas.

Staff Development Training Videos

The following professional development training videos allow teachers to view lessons in primary classrooms that incorporate reasoning as a fundamental component. The videos also offer tips and strategies for helping students effectively communicate their reasoning about mathematics. The accompanying manuals provide reflection questions and activity ideas.

Hersch, S., A. Cameron, M. Dolk, and C. Twomey Fosnot. 2004. *Fostering Children's Mathematical Development, Grades PreK–3 (Resource Package)*. Portsmouth, NH: Heinemann.

Mathematics: Teaching for Understanding. 1989. Vernon Hills, IL: ETA Cuisenaire.

Storeygard, J., R. Corwin, and S. Price. 1995. *Talking Mathematics: Supporting Classroom Discourse*. Portsmouth, NH: Heinemann.

Using Vocabulary and Writing Strategies to Enhance Math Learning, Grades 1–2. 2005. Bellevue, WA: Bureau of Education and Research.

Barnett-Clarke, Carne, and Alma Ramirez, Editors. 2003. *Number Sense and Operations in the Primary Grades: Hard to Teach and Hard to Learn?* Portsmouth, NH: Heinemann.

Baroody, Arthur J. 1993. *Problem Solving, Reasoning, and Communicating (K–8): Helping Children Think Mathematically.* Englewood Cliffs, NJ: Macmillan.

Baroody, Arthur J., and Ronald T. Coslick. 1998. *Fostering Children's Mathematical Power: An Investigative Approach to K–8 Mathematics Instruction.* Mahwah, NJ: Lawrence Erlbaum.

Ben-Hur, Meir. 2006. *Concept-Rich Mathematics Instruction: Building a Strong Foundation for Reasoning and Problem Solving.* Alexandria, VA: Association for Supervision and Curriculum Development.

Beto, Rachel A. 2004. "Assessment and Accountability: Strategies for Inquiry-Style Discussions." *Teaching Children Mathematics* (May): 450–54.

Burns, Marilyn. 1997. "How I Boost My Students' Number Sense." *Instructor* (April): 49–54.

———. 1999. *Writing in Math Class: A Resource for Grades 2–8.* Sausalito, CA: Math Solutions.

———. 2005. "Looking at How Students Reason." *Educational Leadership* (November): 26–31.

Carpenter, Thomas P., Megan L. Franke, and Linda Levi. 2003. *Thinking Mathematically: Integrating Arithmetic and Algebra in Elementary School.* Portsmouth, NH: Heinemann.

Chapin, Suzanne H., and Art Johnson. 2000. *Math Matters: Understanding the Math You Teach, Grades K–6.* Sausalito, CA: Math Solutions.

Chapin, Suzanne H., Catherine O'Connor, and Nancy Canavan Anderson. 2003. *Classroom Discussions: Using Math Talk to Help Students Learn, Grades 1–6.* Sausalito, CA: Math Solutions.

Clement, Lisa L., 2004. "A Model for Understanding, Using, and Connecting Representations." *Teaching Children Mathematics* (September): 97–102.

Clements, Douglas H, and Julie Sarama, ed. 2004. *Engaging Young Children in Mathematics: Standards for Early Childhood Mathematics Education.* Mahwah, NJ: Lawrence Erlbaum Associates.

Copley, Juanita V., ed., 1999. *Mathematics in the Early Years.* Reston, VA: National Council of Teachers of Mathematics; Washington, DC: National Association for the Education of Young Children.

———, J. V., 2000. *The Young Child and Mathematics.* Washington, DC: National Association for the Education of Young Children.

Dacey, Linda Shulman, and Rebeka Eston. 1999. *Growing Mathematical Ideas in Kindergarten*. Sausalito, CA: Math Solutions Publications.

———. 2002. *Show and Tell: Representing and Communicating Mathematical Ideas in K–2 Classrooms*. Sausalito, CA: Math Solutions Publications.

Falkner, Linda Levi, and Thomas P. Carpenter. 1999. "Children's Understanding of Equality: A Foundation for Algebra." *Teaching Children Mathematics* (December): 232–36.

Findell, Carol R., Mary Cavanagh, Linda Dacey, Carole E. Greenes, Linda Jensen Sheffield, and Marian Small. 2004. *Navigating through Problem Solving and Reasoning in Grade 1*. Reston, VA: National Council of Teachers of Mathematics.

Flores, Alfinio. 2002. "How Do Children Know That What They Learn in Mathematics Is True?" *Teaching Children Mathematics* (January): 269–74.

Greenes, Carole. 1999. "Ready to Learn: Developing Young Children's Mathematical Powers." In *Mathematics in the Early Years*, ed. Juanita V. Copley, 39–47. Reston, VA: NCTM; Washington, DC: NAEYC.

Greenes, Carole E., Linda Dacey, Mary Cavanagh, Carol R. Findell, Linda Jensen Sheffield, and Marian Small. 2003. *Navigating through Problem Solving and Reasoning in Prekindergarten—Kindergarten*. Reston, VA: National Council of Teachers of Mathematics.

Greenes, Carole, and Carol Findell. 1999. *Groundworks—Algebraic Thinking—Grade 1*. Chicago, IL: Creative Publications.

Herbert, Kristen, and Rebecca H. Brown. 2000. "Patterns as Tools for Algebraic Reasoning." In *Algebraic Thinking, Grades K–12: Readings from NCTM's School-Based Journals and Other Publications*, ed. Barbara Moses. Reston, VA: National Council of Teachers of Mathematics.

Ittigson, Robin. 2002. "Helping Students Become Mathematically Powerful." *Teaching Children Mathematics* (October): 91–95.

Kallick, Bena, and Ross Brewer. 1997. *How to Assess Problem-Solving Skills in Math*. New York: Scholastic Professional.

Krulik, Stephen, and Jesse A. Rudnick. 1998. *Assessing Reasoning and Problem Solving: A Sourcebook for Elementary School Teachers*. Needham Heights, MA: Allyn and Bacon.

Lampert, Magdalene. 2001. *Teaching Problems and the Problems of Teaching*. New Haven, CT: Yale University Press.

Lederhouse, Jillian N. 2003. "The Power of One-on-One." *Education Leadership* 60 (7): 69–71.

MacGregor, Mollie, and Kaye Stacey. 1999. "A Flying Start to Algebra." *Teaching Children Mathematics* (October): 78–85.

Mitchell, Peter, and Kevin J. Riggs, ed. 2000. *Children's Reasoning and the Mind*. East Sussex, UK: Psychology Press Ltd., Publishers.

National Council of Teachers of Mathematics (NCTM). 2000. *Principles and Standards for School Mathematics*. Reston, VA: National Council of Teachers of Mathematics.

———. 2003. *Mathematics Assessment-A Practical Handbook for Grades K–2*. Reston, VA: NCTM.

———. 2006. *Curriculum Focal Points for Prekindergarten through Grade 8 Mathematics*. Reston, VA: NCTM.

National Research Council. 2001. *Adding It Up: Helping Children Learn Mathematics*. Washington, DC: National Academy Press.

O'Connell, Susan. 2000. *Introduction to Problem Solving: Strategies for the Elementary Math Classroom*. Portsmouth, NH: Heinemann.

Reid, David. 2002. "Describing Reasoning in Early Elementary School Mathematics." *Teaching Children Mathematics* (December): 234–37.

Reys, Robert E., Mary M. Lindquist, Diana V. Lambdin, Nancy L. Smith, and Marilyn N. Suydam. 2004. *Helping Children Learn Mathematics*. 7th ed. Hoboken, NJ: John Wiley and Sons.

Small, Marian, Linda Jensen Sheffield, Mary Cavanagh, Linda Dacey, Carol R. Findell, and Carole E. Greenes. 2004. *Navigating through Problem Solving and Reasoning in Grade 2.* Reston, VA: National Council of Teachers of Mathematics.

Smith, Stephanie Z., and Marvin E. Smith, ed. 2006. *Teachers Engaged in Research: Inquiry into Mathematics Classrooms, Prekindergarten–Grade 2.* Reston, VA: NCTM.

Soares, Joan, Maria L. Blanton, and James J. Kaput. 2005–2006. "Thinking Algebraically Across the Elementary School Curriculum." *Teaching Children Mathematics* (December–January): 228–35.

Starkman, Neal. 2006. "Building a Better Student." *T.H.E. Journal* (September): 41–46.

Stiff, Lee V., ed. 1999. *Developing Mathematical Reasoning in Grades K–12: 1999 Yearbook.* Reston, VA: National Council of Teachers of Mathematics.

Sullivan, Peter, and Pat Lilburn. 2002. *Good Questions for Math Teaching: Why Ask Them and What to Ask (K–6).* Sausalito, CA: Math Solutions.

Trafton, Paul R., and Diane Thiessen. 1997. *Learning Through Problems: Number Sense and Computational Strategies.* Portsmouth, NH: Heinemann.

Van de Walle, John A., and LouAnn H. Lovin. 2006. *Teaching Student-Centered Mathematics, Grades K–3.* Vol. 1. Boston: Pearson Education.

Whitenack, Joy, and Erna Yackel. 2002. "Making Mathematical Arguments in the Primary Grades: The Importance of Explaining and Justifying Ideas." *Teaching Children Mathematics* (May): 524–27.

Whitin, Phyllis, and David J. Whitin. 1998. *Math Is Language Too: Talking and Writing in the Mathematics Classroom.* Reston, VA: National Council of Teachers of Mathematics.

Willoughby, Stephen S. 1997. "Functions from Kindergarten through Sixth Grade." *Teaching Children Mathematics* (February): 197–200.

Yackel, Erna. 1997. "A Foundation for Algebraic Reasoning in the Early Years." *Teaching Children Mathematics* (February): 276–80.

Why Are the Activities on a CD?

At first glance, the CD included with this book appears to be a collection of teaching tools and student activities, much like the activities that appear in many teacher resource books. But instead of taking a book to the copier to copy an activity, with the CD you can simply print off the desired page on your home or work computer. No more standing in line at the copier or struggling to carefully position the book on the copier so you can make a clean copy. And with our busy schedules, we appreciate having activities that are classroom ready and aligned with our math standards.

You may want to simplify some tasks or add complexity to others. When it is appropriate for your students, simply delete some sections for a quick way to simplify or shorten the tasks. This CD gives you much more than a mere set of activities. It gives you the power to create an unlimited array of problems that are suited to your students' interests, needs, and skills. Here are some examples of ways you may want to change the tasks and why. A more complete version of this guide with additional samples for editing the activities can be found on the CD.

Personalizing Tasks or Capitalizing on Students' Interests

The editable CD provides a quick and easy way to personalize math problems. Substituting students' names, the teacher's name, or a favorite restaurant, sports team, or location can immediately engage students. You know the interests of your students. Mentioning their interests in your problems is a great way to increase their enthusiasm for the activities. Think about their favorite activities and simply substitute their interests for those that appear in the problems.

For example, one teacher knew that many of her students spent their summer involved in local activities. She decided to reword the following task to reflect her students' local interest (see the second version of the problem). (*Note:* This type of editing is also important when the problem situation may not be culturally appropriate for your students.)

Name _____

Vacationing with Relatives

Keith travels during summer vacation with his relatives.

They enjoy going to the beach, the lake, the mountains, and the city.

Read the clues to find out where each family member vacations.
- Aunt Terry's sister, Mary, enjoys water.
- Uncle John likes to visit places with tall buildings.
- Uncle Sam likes to visit the coast.

	Aunt Terry	Uncle John	Aunt Mary	Uncle Sam
Beach				
Lake				
Mountains				
City				

Tell how you know what Aunt Terry likes.

_____

_____

_____

_____

_____

Name _____

Summer Vacation

Keith enjoys going places with his relatives during summer vacation.

They enjoy going to the swimming pool, the park, the shopping mall, and the movies.

Read the clues to find out which place each relative prefers.
- Aunt Terry's sister, Mary, enjoys water.
- Uncle John likes to visit places with tall trees.
- Uncle Sam likes to go shopping.

	Aunt Terry	Uncle John	Aunt Mary	Uncle Sam
Pool				
Mall				
Park				
Movies				

Tell how you know what Aunt Terry likes.

_____

_____

_____

_____

Editing the CD to Differentiate Instruction

Modifying Readability of Tasks

Adding some fun details can generate interest and excitement in story problems, but you might prefer to modify some problems for students with limited reading ability. Simply deleting some of the words on the editable CD will result in an easy-to-read version of the same task.

Note: In the second version of the following problem, the statement asking students to explain their answer was revised from the statement on version 1. The lines were also deleted and replaced with a box. Students can now record their explanation of reasoning inside the box.

Name _____

How Many Are Invited?

Jan will soon be eight years old.

She is inviting 12 friends to her birthday party.

She invites two more girls than boys to the party.

Use the comparison circles to help you show how many girls and boys are coming to the party.

Boys	Girls

How many girls will be invited to the party? _____

Explain how you figured it out.

_____

_____

_____

_____

Name _____

How Many Are Invited?

Jan is inviting <u>12</u> friends to her party.

She invites <u>two more girls than boys</u> to the party.

Use the circles to help you show how many girls and boys are coming to the party.

Boys	Girls

How many girls will be invited to the party? _____

Show how you figured it out.

Creating Shortened or Tiered Tasks

While many students are able to move from one task to another, some students benefit from focusing on one task at a time. By simply separating parts of a task, either by cutting the page into two parts or by using the editable CD feature to put the two parts of the task on separate pages, teachers can help focus students on the first part of the task before moving them to the second part. Teachers might choose to provide all students with the first part and then give students the second part after they have completed the first part and had their work checked by the teacher. In the next sample, in which all the information and the question initially appeared on one page together, the space for writing the answer is separated and the lines for writing responses are widened for students who need more writing space.

Name _____

Houses

Ruth, Shannon, Fred, and Todd live on the same street.
Their houses are in a row.

Use the clues to figure out the order of their houses.

Write the children's names under the correct houses.

Clues:
- Ruth's house is between Shannon's house and Fred's house.
- Shannon's house is first.

First Second Third Fourth

Explain how you determined the order of their houses.

_____

_____

_____

_____

_____

Name _____

Houses

Ruth, Shannon, Fred, and Todd live on the same street.
Their houses are in a row.

Use the clues to figure out the order of their houses.

Write the children's names under the correct houses.

Clues:
- Ruth's house is between Shannon's house and Fred's house.
- Shannon's house is first.

First Second Third Fourth

Work with a partner to put the names of the children on paper to help
you solve the problem.

Name _____

Explain how you determined the order of their houses.

_____

_____

_____

_____

_____

Modifying Data

While all students may work on the same problem task, modifying the problem data will allow teachers to create varying versions of the task. Using the editable CD, you can either simplify the data or insert more challenging data including larger numbers.

Name _____

Chapter Books

Terry, Emma, Billy, Jack, and Alan have 15 chapter books altogether.
They each have a different number of books.
Use the clues and the chart to help you figure out how many chapter books each person has.
Jack has only 1 chapter book.
Emma has the most chapter books.
Emma and Billy have 7 chapter books together.
Terry has 1 book less than Alan.

	1 book	2 books	3 books	4 books	5 books
Emma					
Terry					
Billy					
Alan					
Jack					

How did you figure out how many books Billy has?

_____

_____

_____

_____

Name _____

Chapter Books

Terry, Emma, Billy, Jack, and Alan have 20 chapter books altogether.
They each have a different number of books.
Use the clues and the chart to help you figure out how many chapter books each person has.
Jack has only 1 chapter book.
Emma has the most chapter books.
Emma and Billy have 14 chapter books together.
Terry has 1 book less than Alan.

	1 book	2 books	3 books	4 books	10 books
Emma					
Terry					
Billy					
Alan					
Jack					

How did you figure out how many books Billy has?

_____

_____

How many chapter books would the children have altogether if Billy had the same number of books as Emma? Use the back of this paper to explain your reasoning.